JUST OFF THE AISLE

JUST OFF THE AISLE

The Ramblings of a
Catholic Critic

by
Richard A. Duprey

THE NEWMAN PRESS
Westminster, Maryland
1962

First published, 1962

TO THREE MOTHERS—
My Own,
Who bore me;
The Mother of my Children,
Who lovingly puts up with me;
The Mother of God
*Who bears my rebellions and excesses
with Heavenly patience.*

AUTHOR'S NOTE

Much of the material published in this book has previously appeared in whole or in part in *The Critic, The Catholic World,* and Philadelphia's *The Catholic Standard and Times.*

Grateful acknowledgment is made to the following publishers for permission to use material from their publications:

Simon and Schuster, Inc., for *Four Screenplays by Ingmar Bergman.*

Sheed & Ward, for *The Image Industries,* by Wm. Lynch, S.J.

Alfred A. Knopf, Inc., for *The Borstal Boy,* by Brendan Behan.

Porter Sargent, Pulisher, for *The American Sex Revolution,* by Pitrim Sorokin.

America and *Commonweal* magazines for excerpts from editorials.

Contents

Introduction

A great many people today, inside and out of the entertainment world, are deeply concerned about the matter of "Catholic criticism" as regards theatre and the motion pictures. The Catholic is concerned because he is seeking to preserve his ideals in a confusing world—a world where almost nothing seems to make sense from a Christian point of view—and according to the moral code to which he subscribes. The non-Catholic is concerned because he seeks to preserve the arts and his own personal freedom in the face of what seems for all the world like the anachronistic appearance of undiluted Jansenism in Roman collar and cassock. Peculiarly enough, most of these people, Catholics and non-Catholics alike, don't understand what "Catholic criticism" is and what sort of opinions a Catholic reviewer may hold without being burnt on some archbishop's lawn. To almost everyone, the Catholic who writes drama and film criticism is considered a sort of anti-art Bishop Bossuet—a fellow who is out to clean up the arts even if he has to destroy them in the process.

Modern drama and its dramatists have become *anathema* to many Catholics who equate Tennessee Williams and William Inge with Lucifer and Beelzebub. On the other hand, many people in the theatre don't know quite what to make of these "ogre" Catholics. They think (and one can hardly blame them) that Catholics will be deeply offended at the mere mention or depiction of divorce, suicide, or any sexual problem, regardless of treatment.

The lingering image—the disturbing picture impression one all too often receives in thinking of Catholic attitudes toward the arts—is that of a knot of Catholic War Veterans picketing a theatre where some alleged adulteress is playing. Over and above the obvious vulgarity of the procedure one can be led to wonder whether these zealots have ever heard the Gospel about the woman taken in adultery. This image is a disturbing one both to the average citizen who is not a Catholic and to those Catholics who deal in the field of art or who seek to use the arts with any degree of frequency.

As a "Catholic critic"—in the narrowest sense, one who as a Catholic writes for a Catholic periodical—I view the theatre from a ghetto. It is not a physical ghetto nor is it a form of political, economic, or sociological restraint, but it is real and tangible nevertheless. Like all American Catholics I find myself hemmed in by a wall—a strange wall which we have helped the artists of the world to build around us—a wall made up of misunderstandings, prejudices, and suspicion. Mutual suspicion in which we Catholics look askance at the theatre while the theatre trains a wary eye on us. We Catholics have insulated ourselves, to a considerable degree, from the world of art, and the world of art has, quite prudently, turned its back on us.

This book does not come forth as a proposed answer to this difficulty—this embolism of misunderstanding. It is only offered as an initial step in creating some sort of dialogue— some modicum of rapport between the curators of our theatre and the sincere Catholic who all too often appears the hammer-fisted iconoclast.

The approach is not a dogmatic one, but a subjective one and if it seems that the opinions, prejudices, ideals, and interpretations set forth are of a too personal nature, perhaps this in itself will prove enlightening to those who thought that the Catholic critic must follow a party line—a careful system based on the most extreme prudential thinking.

As chairman of a university theatre department and as a Catholic critic—writing a regular column for a major Catholic weekly and sharing the drama critic's seat for a national Catholic magazine—I have sought to expand a series of critical discussions dealing with modern drama and the so-called "Catholic point of view," if indeed such a creature really exists. It is likely that the reader will find the following chapters discursive, opinionated, and at times evasive. This is the price one has to pay when dealing with a college teacher and the reader will further do well to remember George Jean Nathan's famous allegation that a drama critic without prejudices is like a general who refuses to take human life. In reading this book, the reader is twice beset with the pitfall of prejudicial opinion.

Despite all this, I have sought here to write from an honest Catholic viewpoint, with a peculiarly Catholic approach to the nature of man, the basic purpose of art, and the responsibilities of the artist. This is not to say that the approach herein is a philosophical one, for I am not a philosopher nor do I aspire to be one. There is a certain pragmatic approach to my critical writing, for I find it far easier to "feel" in the theatre than to "reason."

There may be, for one who is genuinely seeking light in regard to Catholic criticism, some illumination to be had in examining these pages. The practitioner of theatre who seeks to get a better look at the dull sectarian fellow who peers at him from Row M may discover something of value to him. The sincere and puzzled Catholic who has been led to believe modern drama is purely a cesspool—a squalid vice-ridden thing that the pope would like to exterminate—may discover that even in the theatre God's footprints are to be found. Perhaps the discouraged artist who feels that he cannot write genuinely human plays and maintain some degree of legitimacy as a Catholic may here find at least one friend. All of these possibilities are the merest conjecture and I hereby grant the reader the right to make of me what he will. It's likely that he'll do this with or without my blessing.

I ask but one thing of the reader. Do not open this book looking for answers, for the drama, particularly the modern drama, seeks only to ask questions; and as the dramatists of the world, questioning, open doors in dark places, they find only more questions. This is the price one pays for living, for on this side of death we can never hope for final answers—at least from the hands of the artist. The exciting thing about life is that we have consigned ourselves to mystery and through the theatre, where two and two make twenty-two far oftener than four, we exercise our human right to be surprised, amazed, and initiated into further mysteries.

As a Roman Catholic who believes that faith is but the front hall of revelation, I write with great delight about the modern drama, that great puzzling thing which causes many of my fellow watchers from the ghetto to furrow their brows in perplexity and to purse their lips in indignation. This book may deepen some frowns and pucker a pout or two, but perhaps it is time for a Catholic critic to speak up and try a few new avenues—try chasing up a few other approaches—to seek, as best he can, to close, even by some small fraction of an inch, the great false gap between art and morality.

Chapter One

Background Noise

IF it is true that we Catholics are bound by Christian obligation to become "engaged citizens of the world," applying Christian principles to the problems and provocations of a pluralistic culture, yet living in that culture, partaking of it, sharing in its responsibilities, using it meaningfully, and acting as a leaven within it, then it is similarly true that in one major area we have failed.

In the communication arts, those great and inescapable influences on the life of contemporary man, we Catholics have followed a course of reaction, answering when we imagined ourselves challenged, showing a marked disinterest, suspicion, and downright hostility to anything spoken in the name of the arts. Our Catholic people have manifested little identification with or helpful interest in the arts of communication. The graduates of our schools have demonstrated a marked tendency to lag behind their non-Catholic brethren in making sane and adult evaluations of theatre, motion pictures, television, and fiction, for we have denied them training and filled them with an almost reflex-action sort of uneasiness when they draw near to art in any form.

Sunday after Sunday, our preachers stand forthright and impregnably self-righteous in their pulpits, alleging bad faith to every person in the realm of the theatre, the motion pictures, television, the publishing world, etc., who dares to disagree in any way with their own particular diagnoses of the licit way to achieve artistic wholesomeness.

These pulpit polemicists, armed with the authority the clerical collar gives them, thunder forth half-truths in the name of God, make unchristian allegations regarding the entertainment-makers and their "real" intent and so pervert the public image of Christian truth with the blind energy of their zeal that the world shakes its head sadly and passes us Catholics by, excluding us from the dialogue of those interested in the world of art and anxious to employ it in the "life-enrichment" for which it was intended.

3

Our colleges and our universities, despite contributing to the usual claims that the Church nurtured art through the Dark Ages (a claim one suspects to be quite proper and true despite Catholic prejudices today), have, for the most part, turned the arts *out* and have been noticeably deficient in encouraging them to positive growth. For the most part, these institutions, dedicated to the ideal of broadening the whole man toward his ultimate potential of growth in breadth and depth, have avoided one of the heaviest contributors to this very process of human enrichment. Often pleading poverty for an excuse, which really hides a dogged feeling that the arts are not quite safe, they tend to ignore the whole area, to pretend it is not there and needs no curricular attention. Art is tolerated as an extra-curricular activity under careful control, but is often denied any real encouragement.

In today's "rat-race" of scientific competition, our Catholic colleges, which should husband their unique qualifications to safeguard Christian humanism, have squandered much of their limited resources on becoming shoddy facsimiles of M.I.T., quite forgetting that there is more than one way of rocketing man into the cosmos. They have quite ignored the rocketry of mind, emotion, and spirit that art represents.

Furthermore, the artist of today, the man who genuinely seeks to find man's place in the vast universe, in considering what he hears called "the Catholic position," may justly ask, "What ever happened to charity?" The great theological virtue which, through shattering example, spread the whole truth of Christ's revolution about the world and claimed whole nations for Him, has been hidden away today in an effort to impress, by any charitable *or* uncharitable means at hand, a Christian standard (or the distorted image of a Christian standard) upon a non-Christian society.

The so-called "Catholic position" is a strange and, in a real sense, frightening thing, for though it has no real stature, no rational basis for existence, and no real force within the organizational structure of the Church, it has emerged as a sort of "party line" with thousands of vitriolic letter writers at home, pens poised, ready to do battle for a Philistinism which they misguidedly support as the one true Catholic attitude toward

4

the arts. Operating under the assumption that Catholics have an effective monopoly on justice, honesty, civic virtue, political orthodoxy, and chastity, these people have sought to create an environment in which only a safe, watered down, virtually emasculated art can survive. They have, in the process of such efforts, so perverted the image of Catholic taste and intelligence that the artist tends to think of Catholics as prudish Polyannas lobbying frantically for the utter abolition of self-expression in any form whatsoever, excepting prayer.

For this very reason, a Catholic critic is looked upon with a sort of tolerant amusement and some degree of curiosity by his colleagues who work for the secular press. Further, for the same reason, he is deeply suspected by the theatre itself, and, adding insult to injury, relentlessly checked, week in and week out, by his own readers for any signs of religious or political unorthodoxy or even the faintest sign of "moral laxity." With the whirlpool of liberalism to port and with the rocky shoals of conservatism to starboard, the Catholic critic steers a precarious course between perilous extremes as he seeks to fulfill with some degree of distinction and some degree of honesty the dual function of critic-reviewer to a pragmatic, chaotic modern theatre and a suspicious Catholic public.

At this point it would be well to consider the distinction between "critic" and "reviewer." A reviewer, quite simply, is one who writes essays of a critical nature for a periodical in order to service its readers, enabling them to have the use of his criteria for selecting good and worthwhile entertainment. He merely reports his reactions to the work, trying to be as just and objective as possible in the light of some reasonable norm of excellence, though he is, of course, subject to what he is himself and to a lesser degree to the nature of the publication for which he writes. As a reviewer, his primary responsibility is to his readership and along with his own personal bias must go at least some of the standards of the readers of the publication. Whether his bias or theirs obtrudes or not, the possibility of its presence must most often be taken into account as a factor in reviewing.

The critic, on the other hand, is the custodian of the artistic conscience. As a reviewer talks to the potential audience, the true critic engages in a dialogue with the theatre itself—he addresses the artist and his collaborators. It is his function, as an enlightened student of the art, to evaluate the work of the art medium—theatre or motion pictures in the case of our discussion here—and through his carefully considered critical writings encourage it to greater things, promote self improvement, to cauterize away the shoddy, the inartistic and the crass. His primary responsibility is to the art form and to its improvement. Even though the critics may not agree and even when their judgments, for one reason or another, are suspect, the real artist—the humble man with talent—will go back to his work with as stiff a dose of objectivity as he can take, to re-evaluate and rethink the work on the possibility that the critic may possibly be right. In order truly to be a critic and exercise the full critical function, one must be listened to.

The Catholic critical writer is faced with a genuine limitation in that he has been ignored—genuinely ignored by the world of art because of his known tendency to become enamored of the trees in place of the forest.

It is the function and responsibility of the reviewer-critic to judge. He picks up his tickets, walks into the theatre, takes his seat, and as the curtain is rung up, he observes all that takes place onstage and judges it. Like every other member of the audience, he seeks the truth and beauty that good recreation affords, though in his case it is a more conscious search. Despite the necessity of preserving a certain naïvete, a certain innocence in the theatre so that the play can reach him, he must be a good deal more alert and searching than the average audience member. Most people about to be entertained have only the vaguest idea of what they're looking for while the critic-reviewer, with a pocketful of prejudices, a knowledge of theatre history, and an eye and an ear for technique, goes in knowing almost exactly what he is looking for. Even if he cannot describe it in advance, he is at least well conditioned enough to recognize it when it happens and to be able to describe the process to some extent. Like an ideological counterpart of Pavlov's famous canine, when the bell of theatrical excellence is rung, there is some kind of critical salivation.

6

Often he is surprised by the show and loses whatever misconceptions he may have gained from the advance advertising and show publicity and what he knows of those participating. Regardless, however, of what happens, the valid and worthy critic goes in asking three questions—the basic questions of all intelligent, reasonable, and well-ordered criticism. He asks *"What is the author trying to do?"*, *"How well does the show succeed in achieving that end?"* and *"Should it have been done in the first place?"*

Taking the questions in the order of application, we first suggest that it is the licit option of the playwright to create on his own terms, to contribute to the theatre whatever he wishes. One cannot, for example, justly criticize a Conestoga wagon for not coming equipped with a diesel engine, or a Volkswagen for its failure to look like a Mercedes-Benz. We must first find the aim, the objective, as it is conceived by its creator. Art is, of course, designed for some level of *use* ranging from the spiritual to the physical depending on whether one stands with Aristotle or Brecht, but the nature of this basic intention must emanate first from the artist. Certainly the cobbler who sets out to make a *woman's* shoe need not justify the finished work on the basis of what a *man's* shoe ought to look like. The choice of objective is in the hands of the playwright and in order to go on to the second question of criticism, the critic must approach the first and answer it. The artist decides what the objective will be and then demonstrates it in his work.

In connection with this, it is necessary that the writer somehow manifest what his object is, for the communicativeness that is at the very basis of the theatre is not well served by playing guessing games at the expense of the audience. In "the temple of evidence," as Henri Ghéon once called the theatre, the audience has the right to know the subject of the conversation between themselves and the dramatist. If the author is compelled to tell you what the play means and what it is generally about by means of essays in the newspaper or the playbill, he has initially fallen short in his work. This is true, providing, of course, that the audience is not *completely* made up of congenital idiots incapable of understanding. One may be an individual but the mass audience never is. The audience

7

is not stupid. History proves this, for great plays—those of Shakespeare, Molière, Marlowe, and Shaw—came from theatres of vast popular appeal and when the large "vulgar" audiences heard them and saw them when they were first produced, they loved and understood them. It is entirely likely that the average Elizabethan audience member understood Prince Hamlet far better than all the drama critics who have since written on the subject. The understanding Shakespeare sought was the understanding of the audience in the Globe Theatre *while* the production went on. Anything else brought to the consideration of the play in subsequent years and centuries is outside the real area of dramatic significance and is less theatre criticism than a sort of quasi literary criticism sprouting forth from the leather bindings of library-embalmed plays.

The second question for the critic is, *"How well does the play serve the end of the playwright?"* Has his intention been served both by his own technique, by the refashioning of his original ideal by the director, and in the interpretation of the actors? In other words, if the intention of the play is to show man a symbolic picture of his own suffering nobility as in *Hamlet* or *Oedipus*, has it really been shown? Or if the playwright has sought to be amusing, has he made the grade in comparison with his own era's standards of performance? Are we amused? How amused? This is the question of *technique*. How well has it been executed? Now we pass from the intention of the work to its execution.

As we move on to the third question, we are brought back abruptly to the central discussion in this chapter. We are brought back with a jolt to the question of Catholic criticism, for there are those—many of them—who think there should be *no* third question. They feel that the critic-reviewer and anyone else, for that matter, should keep his distance. They feel strongly that no one has the right to question whether a thing should be done in the first place. They feel that no one has the right to subject the artist to any evaluation of the intrinsic or extrinsic truth and beauty of his material beyond the simple matter of execution. They insist that he should be judged only on how well he and his cooperating artists have done it. Not only would they deny the art itself the right to protect itself from the subjective vision of the irresponsible, egocentric person, but they would deny the whole of society the right to protect itself and the interests of the commonweal. This dangerous point of view suggests that one shouldn't worry a bit about whether the lettuce is wilted or not as long as the salad is prepared with a sense for color and form. Even if it is rotten they would have you see the exquisite care with which it was tossed. It takes no mental giant to see the obvious fallacy of this point of view. Art, like every other good thing, is fashioned for a purpose. It cannot achieve this purpose if it is judged solely on form with no attention at all paid to content. Art serves man—man is not created to serve art.

Casting the shrill objections of the "form-firsters" aside, we do, considering Catholic criticism, ask the question with vigor, *"Should this work have been done?"* Is the material true enough to the nature of life as seen through the eyes of a sincere and responsible artist to warrant its performance? Does the integrity of the artist through technique and conviction render it beautiful? Is the work sincere and communicative and is it endowed with the nobility a man's vision of life may have even if it is confused and questioning? Can we honestly say that it somehow has a "life-enhancing quality" that will profit us? The critic-reviewer must, in order truly to complete his obligation to both parties of his responsibility, answer this third question.

But as he answers this, he must be conscious of a danger. This is the kind of question that the censorial mind asks and answers all too quickly with a facile disregard for the value of art and the importance of its freedom (freedom, that is, not to be confused with license). The critic must not jump to conclusions regarding this question nor attempt to ban things just because he does not agree with them. It is a question which must be based on careful, fair reflection and some degree of knowledge.

The omniscience that some of us are willing—even eager—to assume for ourselves in judging art and the motives of artists is fearsome. We freely impute ill-will, if not positive

9

malevolence to anyone whose work seems dangerous in any way, even as a clear result of our own ignorance.

There is no conflict between art and morality. As a matter of simple fact, one cannot involve oneself in judging a work of art without somehow involving both of these. For too long an artificial gap has been allowed to exist between the positions of artist and moralist. It is an artificial division and a dangerous one.

Eric Gill was once quoted as having said:

> Many prudent men quarrel with art, however good, because many prudent men are prudes. And this quarrel can never be settled until most men of prudence are also artists and most artists are also men of prudence.

Furthermore, as Father William Lynch, S.J. says in his brilliant and provocative book, *The Image Industries:*

> Where it is really art, it is its own censor and as the truest censor of what is really human, it need never be on the defensive against morality and should expect an act of collaboration from the latter, because the goals of the two are the same even though their techniques are so different.

Art is necessary for human life as opposed to life on the purely animal level. Art enables man to gaze at himself and in seeing his own reflection he sees also the image and likeness of His Creator in whose form he has been fashioned. Man suffering, man joyful, man sinful, man triumphing over adversity and pain—in all of these human operations—wherever the creature is depicted as truly rational and truly possessed of free will there is an experience of great value to the emotion, the mind, and the soul of man.

This matter of rationality is all important. Despite Lope de Vega's delightful farce *The Gardener's Dog* (which is really about people), plays are not written about animals. Animals, though delightful companions, difficult enemies, and sources of food and other valuable products, are hardly the true companions of man. Animals, though possessed of some elemental sort of mental power, cannot reason. Their actions are bereft of true interest because there is no real reflection behind them

—they are precipitous and do not come from passion—only instinct. No animal really acts as an individual.

Madmen too, are poor sources of dramatic interest. The actions of a madman follow some pattern that the rational cannot detect. To the sane mind, the actions of a madman spring from perversity and are unexpected and ill motivated.

The unexpected is not an ideal of the theatre. The great plays of antiquity were those based on known legends and the best plays of today at least render the unexpected logical and probable through careful exposition and the development of character motivation through some reasonable pattern of psychology. The great German drama critic Gotthold Ephraim Lessing demanded of the drama a certain "inner probability." A play dealing with one who is mad, or with an animal, loses this inner probability and denies the rational man witnessing the play an opportunity to see himself mirrored upon the stage.

We go to the theatre to see man, recognizable to our own humanity, struggling for goals. Sometimes he chooses good goals and sometimes evil ones. Sometimes he prospers and on other occasions he fails. It is in this human struggle—willing, wanting, striving, hoping—that our interest is kindled. The arts can, and most assuredly do, build character in us when they achieve and maintain their touch with the essential nature of man. In this aspect of artistry they are true and they are beautiful. When truth and beauty are present, morality is never absent.

Chapter Two

"The Catholic Position"

T* the view of many in the professional theatre and for various artists who operate elsewhere in our society, the Catholic is a frightening creature, enthusiastically devoted to the destruction of art. Unfamiliar with the strange historical phenomena which have driven the Catholic ever farther from his own tradition and ever closer to that of Port Royale, that of the Puritan Suppression, and that of a thoroughly winded Victorianism, the non-Catholic is puzzled and upset though upon occasion he joins with his Catholic brother in railing at true offenses against the public good.

At this point it must be stated that there are clearly times when protestation is necessary against that which masquerades as art—open pornography, violent political tractarianism (both right and left), and so-called blasé violence. However, one of the main points is that the artist as well as the moralist has an obligation to cry out in such cases. Both are being plundered.

Clearly, however, the just and honest cries of "Foul," will be ignored if the tendency is to hoot at everything. Society clearly remembers the old tale of the boy who cried wolf once too often. We Catholics have given the world some cause to wonder if we have not cried alarm just a bit too frequently.

For example, in the words of Mulcanny, one of Sean O'Casey's pugnacious characters in *Red Roses For Me:*

Indecent! And what may your eminence's specifications of indecency be? (*Angrily*) Are you catalogued, too, with the Catholic Young Men going about with noses long as a snipe's bill, stripping the gayest rose of its petals in search of a beetle, and sniffing a taint in the freshest breeze blowing in from the sea?

Producers are reluctant to be reviewed by Catholic critic-reviewers. Their reasons are rarely sinister. It is not so much that they want to get away with some filthy trick as many of the sermons and editorials seem to suggest. They feel, most of them, with honesty and sincerity, that the Catholic reviewer comes to the theatre ready and eager to condemn the first vulgar word, the first glimpse of a female knee, the first sinful deed depicted onstage. It is their fear that Mister Catholic Critic will be so indignant at the particulars that he will completely miss the production as a whole and will run forth from their theatre spouting condemnation to all who will listen. It is a source of genuine surprise for many of these men to find a Catholic reviewer who writes honestly and in the genuine Catholic tradition. Often they wonder about Walter Kerr's relationship with his Church or they question the orthodoxy of Richard Hayes of *The Commonweal*.

Commonweal itself, in its editorial columns, took note of this whole unfortunate situation with a 1955 editorial in which the editors commented:

> It is fitting and proper, certainly, that the Church concern itself with public morals. It is neccessary that such an organization as The Legion of Decency exist. But it is unfortunate that Catholics appear always to play the role of philistine—and this they must do for as long as they adopt a narrowly and exclusively moralistic approach to the arts. That they often adopt such an approach, and seem everywhere to urge it, is especially sad, because the Catholic tradition is not a Puritanical one. The Church is the mother of the arts, not their policeman. (*Commonweal*, 62: 219, 20, Je.3, 1955).

This "police" function often seems, in informal discussions with our fellow Catholics, to be the only relationship generally acknowledged between the Church and the art world. The question, "When are we Catholics going to do something about the movies and the theatre?" is so very often asked.

In the realm of the arts, the average American Catholic is, for all the world, like the guest at Lucretia Borgia's dinner party. He sits at the table where the great feast has been spread before him, but he cannot eat as he chokingly inquires of his hostess, "The food looks grand, but when do I get poisoned?" And though all theatrical producers and movie makers do not wear the poison rings of Lucretia, the almost neurotic fear hangs on and we gag most easily at the banquet of art whether Lucretia is about or not.

Often the Catholic has been predisposed to an unnatural and even, on occasion, nearly neurotic suspicion of anything spoken in the name of art. He becomes much like the young child, who first having heard of germs refrains from touching anything for several days until he accustoms himself to the fact that he always runs the risk of infection and he can't lock himself off in some germ-free world. But he is so led, for in the Sunday morning sermon previously mentioned he hears "dirty movies and filthy stage plays" again and again until the phrase becomes one of the slogans by which he lives either denying himself the legitimate pleasures of the theatre *in toto* or saying "to hell with it!" and ignoring the warnings entirely because of their immoderate tone. Similarly, the Catholic school child hears sweeping generalizations about "immoral books and salacious television programs" without being given any norm with which to judge these things. The school Sister who warns the child is in a rather untenable situation herself in that she is fortunate if she has found time to read over her class assignments and get in a bit of spiritual reading. She has no time to catch up on the latest "secular" reading or to study the offerings of television. So no criteria is given along with the condemnatory phrase and the conscientious Catholic must make the difficult application of the Decalogue to the amusement page in the local paper. It's not at all easy!

We Catholics must live in the world and we cannot legislate the arts out of existence. Indeed we should not want to do so from the standpoint of gratitude, for they have played a unique and exciting part in keeping the flame of Faith alive.

In the Age of Faith, from the tenth through the thirteenth centuries, our forefathers who could not read found their lessons of love and religious understanding, of dogma and moral precept, in the art work of the Church. In stained glass, in carved stone, in song, and from the stages of the pageant wagons and the terraced mansions of the Continent, they learned their catechism *and* they learned of Christian joy in the utilization of what little leisure time they found in the grim business of keeping alive. The art of the cathedral and the Christo-centric culture of medieval Europe was not what we modern Catholics would call "safe art." It was vulgar and earthy and even, at times, somewhat obscene. It did not attempt to hide sin away nor did it attempt to fix its gaze only on the brighter aspects of life. The medieval Catholic realized that good art can hardly speak of man if it ignores one of its subject's favorite pastimes, sin. One does not kill or drive away a dragon by refusing to look at him. The dragon gobbles you up whether you see him coming or not. If you hope to get away, you'd better be looking!

The Christian in the Age of Faith saw in *all* the created universe a suitable object for art, for all the world and all the works of man, sacred or profane, are part of God's handiwork, mirroring the terrible act of creation. Our negative thinking which would canonize a piece of alleged art for sheer non-offensiveness would make the medieval Christian feel as though he was dealing with some sort of new-fangled heretic or at least with someone markedly deficient in intelligence and taste. Today our Catholic critics and play and film goers are ready to bless a play or film as long as it does not talk of sin, does not show sympathy for the sinner, does not compromise political orthodoxy, or does not criticize the Church or its ministers. This is utter nonsense and it betrays a shocking blindness to the whole purpose of art.

In the presence of the medieval stage's high-jinks, in the midst of a life of violent contrast, engaging in the Feast of Fools where horse manure was burnt before the high altar, the medieval Christian nodded and grinned to say, "Yes, this is all right and proper, for isn't this a mirror of the whole of creation? All of this goes on and yet God is in His heaven and watches over us all." One may note that it took some considerable time before the custom was effectively banned.

The Catholic tradition is and should be understood as one of a realistic contemplation of the world as it is—as God created it and as man altered it. We cannot clean the whole of creation overnight with scrub brush and bucket. Unlike the incredibly optimistic Communist—the romantic of the modern world who suggests that man can through his own efforts achieve some sort of natural perfection on earth—the Christian knows that man is fated to keep on scrubbing for the rest of his days with little evidence of success for his effort.

As one of the characters in George Bernanos' great Catholic novel *Diary of a Country Priest* says:

> The mistake . . . wasn't to fight dirt, sure enough, but to try to do away with it altogether. As if that were possible! A whole parish is *bound* to be dirty. A whole Christian society's a lot dirtier.

And elsewhere:

> Don't go trying to stop a goat stinking like a goat—a waste of time and a source of despair.

The world and almost every aspect of it has a certain goatishness about it. A Catholic cannot forget that man exists in the grip of a fallen nature and, despite his spiritual redemption, on a natural level his state is still that of Father Adam, driven forth from the Garden in nakedness and shame. If we should, ignoring this, demand a completely scrubbed, absolutely antiseptic depiction of man, we are hiding our eyes from our own real condition. If we should, in our longing for primal innocence, adopt a purely negative, censorial attitude, we'll risk imitating the lady who so feared soiling that she threw the baby out with the bathwater.

The world needs more than a soothing balm on her open sores. She needs salt to heal her. We must look, full faced and with open eyes, at the nature of life. Good art allows us to do this and enriches us even though we do not like what we see. Self-knowledge is often painful but always necessary.

Many critics of the modern arts of the theatre cry out like Marya Mannes for more *Fair Ladys* and they scold the dramatist who would cause us to look at things that are not bright and optimistic. They would have us concentrate on the good things of the world and look away from the horrors. Though we can subscribe at least in part to their thinking and say that the creative artist should not keep his gaze fixed *exclusively* on evil, they too would have us subscribe to something fallacious and misleading.

The artist who suggests that man is *nothing* but a cesspool of vice, a fornicating, rapacious, destructive, foul creature, is really being no more untrue to the arts than the man who says

19

that the human is a purely spiritual being, untainted, above corruption, and capable of existing on nothing but the food of angels. Man is a union of flesh *and* spirit. One who claims he is but one of these and not the other is guilty of a lie, and a lie, whether in art or out in the broader areas of life, is always intrinsically evil.

Art must seek the true nature of man. Our hate for some of the things man does must never blind us to the truth of what he really is. Again quoting from the eminent Jesuit, Father Lynch:

The Catholic must hate sin, but this is only the negative aspect of his vocation. His primary vocation is growth toward the fullness of the reality of Christ. In this growth he cannot fully dispense with the collaboratation of the artist. (*The Image Industries*).

The artist's work is to build *with* the teacher, the theologian, the parent, the confessor, the psychologist, the fellow Christian, a full consciousness of the reality of life in the hearts of men. He is, like every other sincere servant of mankind, a part of the redemptive team and must be allowed full opportunity to play his part. Through the pleasurable sensations of mind and emotion one finds in the theatre, the theatre artist educates man in compassion. He "leads through" the actions and travails of men to a newer and clearer vision of what life is.

The fact that there is undoubtedly a great quantity of faith in the public arts today leads us to the simple-minded conclusion that anyone who defends any aspect of the arts, any artist, or who fails to join in the hysterical cry, "To the stake!" is perverted and playing false as a moral Christian.

There *is*, and make no mistake about it, a measure of dirt in the theatre—a certain degree of falsehood—and a quantity of inherent danger. There is dirt and untruth in these arts just as there is sin in the human heart which the arts seek to depict. The Church, along with many purely human agencies, has been scrubbing away at that heart—that soul—that social identity for centuries. Those agencies are, incidentally, not all Catholic, for we did not invent chastity and have no monopoly on continence.

The Church herself, through her hierarchy, is patient. With

her share of the wisdom and patience of her Divine Head, she knows that we can never completely purge concupiscent man. There is no move afoot in Rome to have the world's confessionals torn down, for sin is a constant to man's fallen state and will continue to be so.

Only recently has it become necessary for the hierarchy to speak up again in regard to an art form. The American bishops issued a recent pastoral letter indicting the recent flood of "bad motion pictures" that have come forth from Hollywood. The bishops did not say *all* the movies being made available at this particular time are bad, nor do they condemn all motion picture producers and distributors as penurious, black-hearted wretches who seek to poison our souls. They merely reiterate in sane, strong terms what they said back in 1934 when the Legion of Decency became morally expedient because of the film producers' failure to enforce their own self-regulatory code. The failure of execution likely goes back to the original lack of reasonableness in the code, but the industry's penchant for skirting or or subverting it seems ludicrous and irresponsible in view of the fact that they promoted it, rendered it more unreasonable than it was first written, and then ratified it. The American bishops have attempted to warn the public that the motion picture makers are lying. They (the motion picture makers) claim a self-regulatory responsibility which they have beyond all shadow of a doubt abandoned.

Never before in the history of civilization has man found so much leisure time available to him. Work-saving devices in the kitchen, the speed of modern transportation, the convenience of modern communication, the increasing mechanization of industry have lightened the tasks—the backbreaking work involved in keeping oneself and one's family alive. Like the ancient Athenians with their slave-based economy, we are, with our mechanical slaves, beset by the critical problem of how to use our leisure time. We seek a "creative leisure," for only the most out-and-out hedonist can justify spending *all* his leisure in purely meaningless relaxation, for we have so much of it today. Man cannot vegetate and sit away all his idle hours nor is he constituted so as to sleep them away. The wide use of leisure is a great challenge to us.

All around us din the voices of the public communication media which seek to entertain us—either selling the entertainment itself or using it to sell some other property. One cannot escape from the "narrative arts," the theatre, television, written fiction, the motion pictures—everywhere we are confronted with some form of the business which takes us on conducted tours of the minds and hearts of our fellows. We go to the movies, to the theatre, watch television plays, read stories, and are somehow touched by this almost every day of our lives. Our problem is to make meaningful and significant use of it all, not merely to screen it for the positively hurtful, and then to swallow the rest unquestioningly. One must approach art with a positive intention of extracting something meaningful, worthwhile, and "life-enhancing."

The recreation the arts offer is not pure escapism. No man can or should seek to escape to the point of completely disengaging himself from his fellow or from life in general. Most Catholics would deny that they are guilty of such an escapist point of view in any aspect of life. However, as an illustration of just this sort of thing, one may note the habitual use of the word "decent" by Catholics considering the narrative arts. We seem to have a fixation on this rather negative word. We find it constantly evident in reviews and editorials, find it in the name of our "watchdog" organizations, and find it recurring again and again in pious conversations.

Donald Duck is decent enough, but a steady dose of Donald Duck day in and day out for a period of months and years would turn anyone into a gibbering idiot and, worse yet, would put him into complete spiritual isolation from mankind. No Christian can afford this, for even the contemplative monk maintains a hold on the world through corporate prayer and by keeping the needs and best interests of human society ever in his intentions. The monk does not sit smiling at the trees all day, but rises in the black hours of early morning to wrestle with the Devil. Decency is not enough. One doesn't eat just anything on the basis of a certain knowledge that it isn't toxic. We are more kind to our stomachs than to our minds and spirits, for we demand of table food that it be

22

tasty and nutritious. Something we seem to care nothing for in our stipulations for art.

A few years ago, in Catholic circles, a most interesting debate erupted in regard to a film called *Say One For Me*. This happened to be another "singing Bing type of thing" with Mister Crosby again filling a turned-around collar. Father Harold Gardiner, S.J., eminent critic and literary editor of *America*, wrote a brilliant editorial attack on the film. In this denunciation, Father Gardiner said the film was, "An artistic—and even moral—abomination among current motion pictures." In his editorial, which was headed, "A Film That Needs Blasting," the priest-critic continued, "Its morality consists in suggesting that if you throw an aura of religion around artistic tripe, anything will be excused. This is a lie."

The movie, which most of the critics—Catholic ones, that is—mildly praised, deals with a priest in a theatrical district who tries to set up a marriage for a nice, clean-cut Catholic girl (Debbie Reynolds type) with a wolf who doesn't want her for exactly that reason. It's all very starry-eyed with everyone living quite happily ever after. Father Gardiner says in his attack published July 11, 1959, "It's time for Catholic critics and movie-goers in general to stand up and say that they don't like films that mask their shoddiness by putting an ingratiating actor in a Roman collar."

In answer to this editorial, William Mooring, the syndicated Catholic movie reviewer whose column appears in dozens of religious periodicals, wrote to *America*:

[Are films like *Say One For Me*] . . . to be disparaged by the new *avant-garde* among the Catholic film commentators . . . or are they to be fairly and constructively reviewed . . . without lofty disdain for the movie tastes of the mass audience? Destructive criticism of the Catholic Press especially, when this seems to value esthetics more highly than morals, cannot fail to discourage future output of screen plays touching on religion. (*America*, Sept. 19, 1959).

Mr. Mooring in the above quote takes it upon himself to protect the movie under fire by inferring that such films "touching upon reliigon" should be encouraged. Father Gardiner made short work of this defense with its reference to "destructive criticism" by stating that the mediocre must be destroyed to make way for the good. With this answer, Father Gardiner emphasizes the occasional dichotomy to be found between the position of reviewer and critic. One who merely reviews has a tendency (especially noteworthy is Mooring's tendency to do just this) to be gentle with almost any work, however bad, as long as it isn't overtly harmful to morals or the beliefs of the reviewer. Even when the work is destitute of any positive value as art, Mooring equates, rather too often, good morals with nonoffensiveness, as though morality were merely the absence of something—a completely negative quality. The position of the critic, on the other hand, is that of a good surgeon who realizes that it is often needful to hurt while curing. He must be ready, and sometimes eager, to cut away the slovenly, the cheap, and the superficial to make way for worthy art. There is, of course, a considerable weight of opinion in the profession of art itself that says, "Don't hurt the producer when he does something relatively cheap and everyday; he's just accumulating money to come up with something really good when he can afford it!" This is a common argument, but those who use it fail to realize that a mask worn long enough becomes the face itself.

Father Gardiner in the short but bitter exchange with the "Plato of Hollywood" makes the very good point that the critic's function is also ". . . to lead at least those who come to him for guidance to realize that they *should not* want shoddy fare; that there is better fare to be had."

There is another point brought to light in the *Say One For Me* skirmish that is perhaps a prime factor in the unfortunate relationship between Catholics and the arts. This is, of course, to be noted in Mooring's divorcement of aesthetics from morals, suggesting that one must be ranked above or below the other. This is a basic ideological barrier between the position of the critic and that of the narrow moralist. Gardiner says, "The reality is that in judging an art form the aesthetic content is as important as the moral; indeed, they fuse into one composite judgment."

This, too, is the position of Father Lynch in *The Image Industries:*

> The moral thinker, whose competence I am trying not to invade in this book, knows with regret that his efforts to be morally discerning in his classifications have led to an unhappy impasse. His largest classification (A-1) frequently contains a set of pictures which are morally harmless, but as works of art or as representations of human sensibility and style are nothing but junk, and, deep down, are an offense to the dignity, the greatness of man.

The whole thing boils down to the question of whether it is the function of the arts merely to titillate the imagination for an hour or two in some utterly inane and valueless situation with no reference to life at all, or is it the function of the arts to elevate—to contribute a certain "life-enhancing" acuity of vision to man's days here on earth, dredging deeper the channels of emotional, intellectual, and spiritual life so as to make him a better, more thoughtful, more compassionate human being?

Today, it becomes the responsibility of every Catholic critic —and indeed for every lay Catholic who is *engagé*—to foster a sane and solid philosophy of art.

Today, we Catholic Christians, reconciled to the world, are urged not to reject it but to become engaged in its transmutation. We are urged to cooperate actively with the second petition of the Lord's Prayer, seeing to it, as best we can within our human limitations, that Christ's kingdom be assured on earth. Likely it cannot be done—we *know* it cannot be done— before Gabriel's trumpet rings in our ears, but we are urged to work at it, to render all things Christian, even if they cannot be rendered perfect. We can't stop the goats from smelling like goats but we can do what we can to see to it that they belong to the right flock. This, of course, does not involve withdrawal, nor does it involve legislating everything dangerous out of existence. It involves, instead, coming to terms with the world—setting up a mediative state—a state of peace from whence a certain grace may spring. In this regard the Catholic drama and film critic can become a heavy contributor to the understanding that must be basic for any minimum of regeneration. Such, however, has not been the case.

Such an attitude barring involvement with the world of men is not entirely new to Christianity, but it is unrealistic and futile. In the early days of the Church there was a relative unanimity of opinion among Christians that those who were members of Christ should not concern themselves with the things of the world: the immanent *Parousia* would preclude the need for a concern with the world—for coming to terms with it. Then as time passed and the Christian discovered with each sunrise that his impatience for the Second Coming would not be served, he began to realize, as Hellenic culture bit by bit became superimposed on the Judaic traditions of the early Church, that the world would, whether he liked it or not, be his concern. He became crucified on a cross of conflicting aims—the vertical movement toward a knowledge of God and a horizontal movement toward humanistic concerns.

Often it seems a sort of heroic thing to stand battered and disdaining in the midst of the world's hurly-burly carnival, but it is a false position and it is far from our own native shore. Unlike our Christian forefathers in the Christo-centric thirteenth century, we stand isolated in the ego-centric twentieth and whether we like it or not we cannot change the standards of our age with law and a bit of resolute picketing.

Rather than this, we must show an appreciation and an understanding of the value of superior art and some indication that we recognize it when we see it. Only then can we hope to gain admission to the councils of art. We must not allow the idea to persist that we are a group "against things," but we must somehow create the opinion, by making it true, that we are *for* things. To be sure, we must adopt a certain degree of vigilance, for the apostle tells us that "life is a warfare" and we know also that the Enemy "goes about like a roaring lion seeking someone to devour." We cannot, however, let our vigilance become unhealthy suspicion which blinds our eyes to the beauties of this world that God has created for us. It is a fault of great ingratitude that causes us to avert our eyes from God's tracks in nature and refuse to look upon the good things He has fashioned.

The critic is not a keeper of the conscience of his readers. Even the reviewer cannot be this despite the fact that his area of responsibility involves the audience in a most direct way. The responsibilities of the individual in this regard are clear. Man is the keeper of his own conscience and it is not for another person, regardless of who he is and the degree of his theological competence, to *dictate* in matters of conscience. One must guard himself from evil, making use of the teachings of the Church in regard to principles of faith and morals. But there is no substitute, no short cut, no easy way to a sound, sure conscience. Individual responsibility remains intact. The reviewer can only taste the potion and report on what it tastes like to him. His report cannot become a command either to drink or to abstain. The critic-reviewer has discharged his responsibility when he tells the audience member what he will find there at the theatre, if he has any reason to think it will constitute a serious danger for his normal adult readership.

Sometimes in this regard the Catholic critical writer operates under great pressure. Perhaps no group of critics has a more suspicious readership, intent on sniffing out the smallest hint of laxity. The Catholic layman is a prolific letter-writer, and often, in his misguided zeal, the layman is eager to conduct the reviewer to the stake for being only as Catholic as the Church herself. Of course this suspicion is primarily directed against the lay critic, for the Catholic layman in his commendable veneration for the exalted spiritual state of the priestly life feels that laymen in any field touching ever so slightly on the moral order lack authority.

Of course the priest-critic is not considered sacrosanct in this regard, for in some circles he too renders himself suspect when he dabbles in the "nasty, suspicious world of art." It is obvious in studying Catholic critics and criticism that the priest writer tends to be somewhat more liberal and just than his lay counterpart. I've heard it said, and it sounds likely, that the priest can get away with much less kow-towing to the censorial, Puritan-tainted mentality of his fellow Catholics.

So all of this outlines the problem. How can we maintain Catholic reviewing as an effective guard for those who wish to

avoid proximate occasions of sin and/or wasteful, boring
bits of trivia, and at the same time maintain respect for art and
critical effectiveness? It is time that we American Catholics
become fully cognizant of the rights and obligations that are
properly ours in this culture in which we live. Only through
judicious, knowledgeable, and fair criticism may we gain admission to the councils of art.

Chapter Three

Enter the Catholic Critic

"Catholic criticism" in the United States seems to have been launched on May 8, 1909, when Conde S. Pallen came up with a rather constructive and fairly professional discussion of the state of the Broadway theatre in the pages of *America*, the Jesuit weekly.

At that particular time it seemed that *America* deemed it advisable to offer periodic—or we might say spasmodic—commentaries on the Broadway scene as a result of their suspicion that the secular reviewers of New York were somehow "in cahoots" with the various producers around town. It was thought that *America*, through an occasional review or roundup, might add a little objectivity to the critical picture.

On September 18 of the same year, Pallen came up with another column in which he idealistically suggested that the stage and those who controlled it should seek to become "a moral force in the community."

At the time this might very well have sounded even more naive than it does today in that the theatre was still then very much in the shadow of the great battle of the syndicates that nearly tore the theatre apart around the turn of the century. During this no-quarter fight, the realtor-producers of the day —Shubert Brothers *vs.* Frohman and associates—slugged it out for commercial control of the American stage. This was in no sense an artistic battle, but a matter of theatre buildings, of contracts, and of trade. Though by 1909 things were pretty well resolved in favor of the Shubert kingdom and the theatre had oddly enough survived the trauma, no one in the theatre could have then conceived of even so much as an "artistic" posture for it, much less a "moral" one.

Another interesting note in Pallen's early work for *America* may be found in his statement, "There is no reason why clean business cannot be good business." One can easily see that even then the question was one of "cleanness" or "uncleanness."

For some time *America* moved along, making occasional

critical forays into the area of theatre—now and then considering the artistic as well as the moral implications of the theatre, but never making any really serious attempt, it would seem, to come to grips with the aesthetic *or* moral arguments beyond a certain superficial level that one can hardly call criticism.

In October of 1916, the even then venerable *Catholic World* printed an article called "Sincerity and the Modern Drama." In this somewhat remarkable essay, Thomas J. Gerrard strongly advocated sexual censorship for stage plays, suggesting that the criteria for deletion should be based on that which in any sense shocks a well-bred young lady of seventeen or eighteen years. Though according to our lights in the contemporary world this seems prudent to the point of being ludicrous, it may be significant to note that no great outcry was raised about the article. At the time it perhaps seemed rather sensible.

The World didn't maintain this position for any length of time, however, for in 1920 the essays of Euphemia van Rensselaer Wyatt began to appear in *The World* and though it was some time before the lively and erudite Mrs. Wyatt began appearing as a regular drama columnist in *The World*, her pieces bore the hallmark of genuine criticism. She was neither a moralist nor a mere reviewer, but attempted modestly to advise the theatre on the artistic worth of its product. She manifested a genuine regard for the importance of art when, all too often, Catholics writing about the theatre treated it with even more crass disdain than the men who sought to commercialize and debase it.

It wasn't until 1924 that regular criticism by a professional reviewer began appearing in a national Catholic publication. When the Calvert Associates were formed and *The Commonweal* was born, Richard Dana Skinner, formerly of the editorial staff of *The Boston Herald*, began a more or less regular column of theatrical comment.

Unlike most of those periodically writing for Catholic publications at the time, Skinner was a liberal (as one would expect of a *Commonweal* critic) whose distaste for censorship and the censorial mind provided an interesting and effective precedent for such critics as Walter Kerr and Richard Hayes who were later to write drama columns for the same outspoken publication. Skinner said, "You cannot have just censorship without having first a recognized and accepted ethical code. From this fact there is no possible escape." Skinner compared censorship to a boomerang which ultimately comes back to strike down those who support it.

Around the same time that Skinner became regular with his publication, *America* too became concerned with drama reviews and Elizabeth Jordan began doing occasional reviews of plays, though for the first months her policy was for the most part to ignore the "dirty" and to praise "the clean." Even in the manner of her phrasing, it may be clearly seen that, unlike Skinner, her concern was purely a moral one.

And so it went. Slowly, cautiously, the various Catholic magazines, weekly and monthly, began reviewing. First it was the stage and then the expanding influence of the motion pictures and some ecclesiastical concern with their influence led to the addition of film criticism.

In October of 1934, Richard Dana Skinner retired as drama critic for the *Commonweal* and with his departure the Catholic press lost its first genuine drama critic. He was the first really to succeed as a critic in the fullest sense of the word and when he died in November of 1941, great acknowledgment of his gifts was made by theatre people as well as those of the Catholic press.

Today, most of the major Catholic periodicals in the United States maintain drama and film critics. *America* employs both Theophilus Lewis, a fine critic formerly with the *Interracial Review*, who covers the stage, and Moira Walsh, who handles films. At the *Commonweal*, the team is Richard Gilman and Philip Hartung. Both these weekly reviews attempt to review almost everything significant opening in the New York metropolitan area, as does the monthly *Sign*, which has one reviewer, Jerry Cotter, covering both stage and screen.

The other magazines are less regular in their critical offerings, with the *Catholic World*, which used to carry monthly critical rundowns on both media, now concentrating on a single "Play of the Month" with a rotating panel of reviewers, and *The Critic* concentrating on articles plus regular columns by Leo Brady, their theatre man, and John E. Fitzgerald, who also contributes film reviews to the *Sunday Visitor* papers.

Jubilee's Associate Editor, Wilfried Sheed, turns out reasonably regular pieces, primarily on the cinema, while Ed Fischer of *Ave Maria* touches all bases in his column, with discussion of theatre, motion pictures, and television.

Many of the diocesan weeklies, too, offer criticism—much of it the syndicated work of a man named William Mooring who handles films from Hollywood.

This is the picture today with reviewers ranging from Sheed and Richard Gilman on the sophisticated left to Cotter and Mooring on the prudential right. Between these extremes range a variety of sorts and shades of critical opinion, but it is evident that those of the left gain their following from the relatively small, culturally oriented, readerships of their somewhat specialized publications, while those on the right are with mass circulation publications and write with confidence, characterizing themselves as champions of the so-called "Catholic point-of-view."

In this connection, one cannot doubt that Cotter and Mooring *do* speak for the majority of American Catholics. As reviewers, these two men at the extreme prudential end of the scale wield great influence. Their critical influence is, however, anything but assured. The people of the theatre and the films are largely unaware of the limited circulation liberal publications of the Catholic press and ignore the "rightists" as "sin-busters" rather than as valid critics.

Perhaps the most conspicuous of all recent Catholic critics—the one most regarded and listened to by the theatre itself—is Walter Kerr, whose critical pieces attracted considerable attention even when he wrote for the *Commonweal*. Kerr, now the highly regarded, much-quoted critic for the *New York Herald Tribune*, distinguished himself, even before his departure from *Commonweal*, by realizing and vociferously communicating the fact that art and morality have no quarrel. Kerr's reviews were knowledgeable, well written, highly professional, and eminently fair. To those in the theatre, however, it seemed incredible that Kerr, an honest critic of the arts, could retain legitimacy as a Roman Catholic.

Regardless of the influence of the various Catholic reviewers operating across the country, the most often discussed aspect of Catholicism's relationship with the narrative arts is the matter of the Legion of Decency. Even in Catholic circles there is great disagreement in regard to the Legion—its nature, its aims, its value.

The Legion of Decency was born in April of 1934 as the result of a growing dissatisfaction on the part of the American Catholic hierarchy with the manner in which the American film industry was implementing its own self-regulatory Film Production Code. The Code, adopted by the producers in February of 1930, was ratified and "put into operation" in March of the same year. The Code, drawn up by Father Daniel A. Lord, S.J., and Martin Quigley and extensively amended by the Producer's Association was to form the basis for a *defense* against the forces which were seeking legal censorship to cut the flood of films dealing with sex and violence. The thinking was that the forces of censorship could only be kept at arm's length if the industry adopted some method of self-regulation.

The Code has come in for extensive criticism in the years since its inception and for the most part one can agree that it is as defective an instrument as it is a subverted one. Nevertheless, even in failure to observe it, the producers have employed it as a refuge against censorial legislation. Their argument is that censorship is largely unnecessary, for we police our own work. Of course, no one really takes this argument seriously and now and then some individual or group has the courage to point out to the producers that their refuge is made of straw and if they don't look out someone will come along and blow the straw house down. All too often, the group warning the producers of this are accused of favoring censorship. An excellent example of this came to light just recently when the retiring Episcopal chairman for TV and Motion Pictures and the committee of the National Catholic Welfare Conference, which supervises the Legion, made just such a warning to the industry. Bishop McNulty warned that the continued failure of producers to police their own material— to clean up their own mess—would in all probability result in legal censorship. The bishop referred to legal censorship as an unfortunate and undesirable result and clearly demonstrated in the text of this statement that such censorship is to be abhorred. Unfortunately, however, movie critics for the secular press, people in the film industry, and an unfortunately large number of Catholics completely misinterpreted the bishop's message and accused Bishop McNulty of favoring "governmental gag." It seems that this is ever the story. The general Catholic consensus or the radical work of certain individuals so colors the atmosphere that when a responsible statement is made by a fair-minded Catholic, no one is ready to listen.

Recently, the Legion has broadened its approach to the motion picture art form and has considered something of the aesthetic implications of films. To be sure, there are still films in the A1 category which are so lacking in art and taste that they are an offense to human intelligence and sensitivity. The special categories, however, which treat of films that require some further explanation beyond that afforded by the simple categorization normally given, represent a real step forward, and the Legion has been extremely just in its use of the special category for such works as *Suddenly Last Summer* and *La Dolce Vita*.

Catholic reviewing in the United States has never really been included in Catholic publications for aesthetic reasons except in the case of periodicals like *The Critic*, whose whole *raison d'etre* is to foster a revival of Catholic culture, and *Jubilee*, *Commonweal*, and *America*. For the most part (and there are a *few* other exclusions perhaps) the reviews have been included to provide a moral safeguard—a sort of heavenly yardstick to protect those in need of protection. In seeking to accomplish only this, we have perhaps been somewhat selfish and shortsighted. We have only blinded our eyes to the offensive and not really tried to transmute it for the betterment of all. It was more a matter of keeping ourselves from it or in some cases a matter of boycotting things out of existence. Never, or almost never, have we tried really to guide the art form to a higher level of achievement.

In so limiting our aims, we may have kept some souls untainted, but perhaps our efforts have not been as efficacious as we have thought them. Surely those disposed to piety have avoided certain entertainment for fear of contamination. The majority of these people would likely never have gone anyway. Then a certain number of average, now-and-then theatre-goers may have been kept out of the theatres by the moral indictments of our Catholic reviewers, but one can only guess at the number of times such reviews have piqued our interest and we have gone to the theatre to see what all the shouting was about. Certainly some of our Catholic reviewers manifest so low a boiling point in regard to "shock" that almost anyone sophisticated enough to know how to buy a theatre ticket would consider himself a bit better able to slough off the moral dangers than said writer. I don't defend this attitude necessarily, but I surely recognize it. Whenever the reviewer makes a particular point of the moral content of a production, unless the level is abysmally low, there's a stampede. It has something to do with the old saw that "Forbidden fruit tastes the sweetest."

But what of the long range view? What of the business of real forceful drama criticism which presumably improves the art itself? Don't we have a responsibility in this area too?

I think we have. I think we have as citizens of a nation—partakers of and sharers in a culture—an obligation to contribute to the betterment of that culture. We have an obligation to help ourselves and our fellow citizens to gain a fuller measure of humanity—a measure of true life enrichment—from the arts. This is an area in which we Catholics seem uniquely well qualified to lend a hand, *if*—and it's a great big "if"—we place ourselves a little more carefully in tune with our *real* cultural heritage, our *true* traditions, and not that peculiarly narrow brand of rigorism that has all too long, here in America, clung to our public image.

Chapter Four

To the Barricades

The Modern Theatre

TODAY in our university theatres, our "Festival" theatres, our "community theatres," and the various other non-commercial operations we call "tributary theatre" we have stuck pretty much to either the passé sex comedy of "Broadway's worst" or we have gone off on a flyer into the world of classic drama with Shakespeare, the Greeks, and various other great works of antiquity. In short, we have become conservative and sometimes sickly green nostalgic.

In sitting enraptured before the genius of a Shakespeare, an Aeschylus, a Molière, or a Marlowe, it is easy and mildly satisfying to shake the head and mourn for their kind unhappily planted in the grave, never to pen another immortal line. We view them with a sort of nostalgia and agree that their distinguished kind will never walk the boards again. We sneer at the dramatists who are and at all the generations to come after and say, "There'll never be another Shakespeare."

Whether this is true or not, we too easily forget that the ancients and the not-so-ancients were writing for their own times, for a specific audience, and for a particular kind of stage. They were not beset with the problems of playwrights torn between the natural wish to write for their own times and the rather arbitrary and artificial objective of writing for generations unborn. They did not have to speak for a multitude of disparate audiences who have little or no agreement in any area, philosophy, taste, interest, or anything else for that matter. They did not create their works for a vague and all-embracing style of staging and an anonymous company to be drawn together after the work is accepted for production. It's little wonder that the modern playwright founders by writing coterie drama or plays so watered-down to please everyone that they seem little more than simple-minded slush.

This, of course, is the enigma of the modern theatre: shall we please a few of the people occasionally or try to please all of the people all of the time? Shakespeare and the other greats of the past, writing for another age and another society, don't really have the answers for us because they never *really* had to face the problem the way our modern dramatists do. Though every age has an element of dissident opinion, each wrote for a *consensus*—a collective agreement.

Though man remains a universal, new times require new answers—new means and methods. We are currently facing a period of transition in our own theatre just as we are facing mind-numbing changes in the era our theatre mirrors. Because our own minds, spirits, and emotions are so staggered by the enormity of these changes and because at every turn we seek to understand their implications better in terms of our humanity, we turn to the theatre again as one of the valuable sources of enlightenment available to us.

Typically enough, when man becomes puzzled—when he seeks to consolidate new gains, new opportunities, to face up to new challenges—he transmutes his old girl friend, the theatre, to a more dignified and practical use than that of a mere escapist diversion. He uses her then like a boy scout compass to orient himself on a sea of perplexity. He demands that she point out for him the true north of aspiration and, if the needle has rusted from neglect and lack of use, he tosses the old theatre aside and takes a new one or he makes the old one over to serve his need.

This is what we are experiencing today as we once again erect the barricades of artistic revolution in the street and our own theatre struggles to afford us the orientation we so gravely need.

In the void left by the withering of inconsequential comedy, that stale meringue of a purely escapist theatre: the modern musical, the practitioners of "Shock theatre" (the *avant gardists* who will be discussed in a later chapter), and those who follow, however fitfully, the "epic theatre" of Central Europe have marshalled their forces. They have sought popular favor while our "boulevard theatre" retreats to a few inexpensive productions like *Come Blow Your Horn* and others of that ilk. This initially is the pattern of revolt in today's theatre and though it is fast happening under our noses many of us are more interested in contemplating our navels and dreaming of the severed *umbilicus* that links us to our theatrical past.

The realistic theatre of just yesterday, reluctantly packing its bags for the short trip to TV and the longer trip to oblivion, was not born without pain and revolt either, and it is well that we remember from whence it came. In order to understand better the sweeping changes our contemporary stage is undergoing, we must discover something of the change that brought the realistic theatre of our times and our fathers' times into being.

It is fascinating to contemplate the cyclical nature of theatre (like all human history) as it swings back and forth between one extreme and the other, as it goes from a profound concern with the creature man to an almost total irrelevancy and then back again to answer his need in a new and different age.

The so-called modern theatre, the theatre we are slowly peeling from us like a dirty shirt, was born rather triumphantly in the late nineteenth century.

When Émile Zola's "Preface to Thérèse Racquin" appeared in 1873 and took its place as the "Communist Manifesto" of the new naturalistic-realistic theatre, the art had drifted far away from a true concern with the needs of contemporary man. With the evolution of the new sciences of man, with a filtering down to the masses of a new consciousness of their hunger, their thirst, and their hope for a better life, it became obvious that the nineteenth century theatre—a theatre of sentiment and polite charm, of spurious excitement and pat situation—had little to offer. Zola as one of the more outspoken of many dissidents wrote:

I am merely expressing my profound conviction—upon which I particularly insist—that the experimental and scientific spirit of the century will enter the domain of drama and that in it lies its only possible salvation. (Barrett Clark, *European Theories of the Drama*).

He referred to the melodrama which had taken hold of the stage during most of the nineteenth and a good portion of the eighteenth century as "the bourgeois offspring of the romantic drama" and manifested contempt for a drama that sought to "play" rather than to "live." Zola and those he spoke for and ultimately inspired had become sick of a clatrap-laden theatre with a bald, sloppy artifice that seemed to have little or no relationship with life. Through the renowned *Théâtre Libre* of Paris, founded by a gas company clerk, André Antoine, and through the other "Free Theatres" (Otto Brahm's *Freie Buhne* in Germany and the Moscow Art Theatre of Stanislavski and Nemirovich-Danchenko), the theatre of our Western civilization became so enamored of "sincerity" and "relevance" that for a time, admittedly brief, our theatre became subject to a dictatorship of accuracy. For example, Antoine rehearsed his cast in a four-walled, completely enclosed set before deciding which wall to strip away. America's David Belasco later provided even more preposterous examples of the business of realism.

It didn't take long for anti-naturalism to come along and for romanticism to fight back and the naturalistic-realistic experiment was short-lived in its purest form. The idea that real life could be communicated by a photographic view, that by holding up "a bleeding slice of life" an audience could be shown man's *real* nature, was attacked by all variety of artists who saw through the utter fallacy of this. However, even as it became compromised from the extreme ideals of its first revolutionaries, the idea of *realism* persisted as a norm in our own theatre. Particularly in America, through the bold experiments of such companies as the Group Theatre and its natural child, The Actor's Studio, we have been strongly influenced by its strictures, and the question of whether the actor should *imitate* or *be* is a question that is often asked in our theoretical writings and in the acting "how to do it texts." We have created several generations of literal-minded playgoers who could put up with the naturalistic excess of a David Belasco (infamous for having purchased a Child's restaurant for placement onstage) or the uncommunicativeness of the "Method" school of acting. These are the folk who almost unconsciously time exits to see if the actor *really* had time to do what he said he would do offstage.

This has been the mainstream of our theatrical development in the present century with the "fly-on-the-wall" school of drama maintaining a certain majority superiority over other efforts. Ibsen and Chekhov, perhaps the two shadows under which the modern theatre developed, heavily influenced us

44

toward representational drama in which we are encouraged to forget that this is the theatre—these are actors—this is make-believe—and to admit, at least on a certain level, that this is actually taking place. Most of us have grown up to this kind of theatre unless we, like most men, have forsaken the theatre for the sports arenas or the Western novels and TV shows, those last holdouts of the romantic spirit.

There were certain areas of revolt. Here in the United States, Thornton Wilder, with a truly eclectic spirit and a profound knowledge of other theatres and other cultures, broke free with his richly evocative "presentational" theatre in which we are encouraged to break away from the literalness of Zola and Ibsen and to freewheel on the highway of imagination. With Wilder, too, there came a powerful and deeply Christian answer to the thinking of Zola and those who followed his theory that man is merely tossed about by forces beyond his control—a creature of no will, subject to neither reason nor self control. Wilder found a great deal of resistance at first and it's altogether likely that his eventual success was not so much due to his refreshing use of convention or his wholesome philosophy as it was to his fantastic ability to evoke the nostalgic images of past happiness—his knowledge of "strawberry phosphates," his memories of horse cars and of the sound of a lonesome morning milk train whistling through the empty hours before dawn.

But there were other attempts too—earlier ones. In Germany and elsewhere in central Europe, other answers were found to bring the bankrupt tradition of melodramatic mush into touch with life. Wedekind, Capeck, Toller, Sternheim and others writing strange, spookily significant plays which sought "a reality beyond reality" were making inroads into the "Free Theatre" revolution. Creating what was called the "Expressionistic Theatre" they abandoned the restricting literalness of Zola's crowd and the "fourth wall" limitation of Ibsen, and they sought through images, through theatrical artifice, a new kind of relevance to the psychological man whose discovery fascinated them as it had the distinguished opposition. These men were, in a sense, the spiritual and artistic children of August Strindberg, whose psychological probing gave a sort

45

of instinctive precedent for their own efforts in the same direction. They, too, sought, in their own chaotic area of the world, to set the ledger straight—to develop a dramatic tool that would be useful to the philosophically fractioned man of the emerging twentieth century. Like an anarchistic bomb squad they attacked the theatre of their day, but unlike today's *avant gardists*, they came bearing the burden of their own talent and they replaced the structures they destroyed with a comprehensible drama of some consequence.

This is essentially the background against which our present-day theatre appeared. It has continued into the dissonant present as well, for these forces—all of them—are still in one respect or another with us today. We are fighting half a dozen revolutions simultaneously and thrashing about trying to find the new theatre—the one that will in turn meet our needs as Zola's inspiration *helped* for a time to meet his. We are divorcing ourselves from realism. We are maintaining the divorce of ourselves and our stage from purely romantic vehicles with their oversized concept of man and their wild dreaming. We are trying to control the burgeoning musical which threatens from time to time to cannibalize the "straight" play. We are fighting to build a theatre of intellect and illumination in place of a theatre of sentiment.

In short, here in the Space Age we are forced to search for a theatre which can manifest that there are other ways to vault into the heavens beside that which involves a rocket booster. We must find a dramatic equation which answers the needs of our troubled times. There is no easy answer that will find us the theatre we need.

The problem falls largely upon the shoulders of the playwright. Our theatre today is immensely competent. We have brilliant directors, gifted designers, and skilled actors. However, in the collaborative business of theatrical creation, the playwright comes first. He supplies the initial impetus and the responsibility of regenerating a theatre ultimately goes back to the playwright.

It has been estimated that over ten thousand Americans write and submit a play each year to some publisher, producer, agent, or other party. To be sure, one is to be commended for having had the fortitude to write a play at all, for the play is likely the most difficult of all forms of writing—synthesizing as it does, all the great arts: the dance, music, the spoken word, literature, and sculpture.

It is a staggering task to grind out more than one hundred typewritten pages of words and actions for "two hours' traffic on the stage." Talking about writing a play and forcing oneself actually to write one are two vastly different things; and good, bad, or indifferent, the man who has finished a play has achieved a mighty task. This is all to the good, for the business of writing a script, whether it's produced or not, can be grandly educational in that it forces one to think out and develop a sustained pattern of thought for some period of time.

This is not to say that the playwright's task is a matter of logic or method, however, for the fascination of the theatre is the mystery of the art—the glorious fact that the answer is always, when the magic works, larger than the sums of the ingredients. The dramatist opens closed doors not to find answers but to loose more questions. There's a tremendous amount of mystery and a glorious sort of confusion to writing a play and the man who tries to write one by formula would do better to answer an advertisement for technical writers in the business section of the Sunday *Times*.

There are other serious problems to be met in evolving the revolutionary new playwrights we need. It can, for instance, be safely conjectured that in the background of most of us there lurks a curious tendency to write for posterity. We try to write the great play for the future, one that will read well two hundred years hence, and as a result, we fail to write for today's theatre. The theatre is, when you come right down to it (and you have to come right down to it, if you want to write for it) the art of the immediate. Everything that is created in the theatre today is written on water. Almost as soon as it is done, it disappears—never to be recaptured in precisely the same way again.

The playwright must write in terms that will be understood

by his audience. If the plays are universal enough to last, so much the better. But the primary obligation is to entertain, to recreate, to thrill audiences in the playwright's own day.

There are all sorts of obstacles in the aspiring playwright's path over and above his "posterity complex." One of the most difficult to overcome in our times, with education worshipped like some sacred cow, is what one might call the literary stumbling block. This common problem appears as a defect in a great deal of the work produced in the last twenty-five or thirty years. After generations of classroom discussion, this problem is the theatrical heresy that claims that the play is just another form of literature and must be guided by its rules and traditions. Bad attempts at verse drama, for an awful example, in our prose age, have crippled many a potential playwright before he ever had a chance to spread his wings. Academic discussions of drama are often the salt under the playwright's tail.

A play is *not* a mere exercise in words, but rather a recipe for a visual-aural experience in which the living actors will "act" a situation before an audience. It is downright unfortunate that the dramatist must commit his initial concept to the medium of written words in order to preserve it until it is produced. It is no semantic accident that we go to *see* a play. One never speaks of going to *hear* a play (not even a musical), although many a writer reacts in his work as though this were the case, making each character ascend a soapbox at least once during the play and regale the audiences' ears with all sorts of platitudes.

Another great problem in the evolution of a satisfactory modern drama is our playwright's ignorance of form. Because today's would-be dramatist rarely works in or around the theatre, he doesn't know its peculiarities and its unique demands. He doesn't know how to use the great machine that is the stage, nor does he have any idea of how best to wield his great tool, the actor.

There's a reason for this. There is in this area a cold-hearted reality in the American theatre which can't be blamed on poor Mister Playwright. In order to produce, a playwright needs a stage and a company. This is a simple axiom that even the most cursory study of theatre history will support. A playwright learns his craft in the theatre. Take the greats, starting with the Greeks, running through the Elizabethans, those who wrote the great Renaissance drama in France, and on to the modern greats: Shaw, O'Casey, Giraudoux, Brecht and all the rest. They wrote plays for production and were regularly produced. For the most part these men knew in advance the company, the stage, the players, and the audiences for which they wrote. They made their mistakes and they achieved their triumphs on the boards and not on the kitchen table.

In our theatre there is a genuine reluctance to do really new material. Broadway doesn't feel that it's in a position to take chances (though it's obviously unavoidable) and in the so-called original material of the commercial theatre one finds a tremendous bulk of adaptation from commercial successes in other media of art. The educational theatres are even afraid of new scripts and only at the rare school can the visionary teacher talk the students into real adventure promoting the works of new playwrights or striking out in new artistic directions. The community theatre is similarly afraid to forsake what they deem "the tried and true" and the festival theatres are reserved for past triumphs. As a result, the aspiring, experimental playwright is hard pressed for a classroom in which to learn his craft. He finds nowhere to grow.

The professional theatre with its stumbling makes it even more difficult, and all too often the producer with his abysmal lack of good taste further confuses the whole pointless dance of confusion.

A final problem besetting the dramatist who would solve the theatrical dilemma of today and follow in the tracks of the greats is his failure to realize that great subtlety and deep metaphysical meaning are often completely missed by the audiences watching the play speed quickly by for the first time. He doesn't know how to use his chosen medium so that it may be understood and appreciated and so his typed script—the work into which he puts so much of himself—remains unused, stillborn, pickled in its embryonic, unproduced state.

Here lies the problem and Shakespeare, the patron saint of playwriting for the English-speaking world, is less help than booby trap. Similarly the other great masters can lead us astray as often as they can put us on the right track. For with all the *cultus* goes the positive danger of a literary veneration of our theatre's past and the great temptation to word baths of poetic profundity. We see and hear the work of a man (taking Shakespeare here) writing for a society still clad in the relatively seamless robe of Christianity and for a fluid stage abounding in imagination and convention. In the warm glow of his greatness it's all too easy to slip into the beguiling error of thinking we should do as he did, think as he thought, and succeed as he succeeded. It's a dangerous sort of assumption.

We run the risk of turning our theatre into a great pillar of salt—frozen like Lot's wife on the spot where we stand. Our complacency at finding great drama in history only to repeat it over and over again in our modern playhouses will divert us away from the shortcomings of our own poor theatre, nailed to a cross of disparate ideologies, buffeted by fads, and flayed by the wild confusion of today's revolutionary madness.

Chapter Five

Quest

In the Footprints of Strindberg

It is inevitable that in an age where faith is overlooked—passed over with a certain wry contempt—artists will spring forth who through their grotesqueries will seek answers to questions posed by faith's absence and will attempt to plumb mysteries that faith itself leaves unexplored. It is interesting to think that God has set these "gargoyles" high on the rooftops of the cathedral that is His creation so that they may drain off the turbid waters that from time to time collect there. Though many such have become the objects of bitter controversy in our century and have been derided as "prophets of doom" and "the new muckrakers," they fulfill a priceless function and are a vital part of our lives here in the Babel of the Twentieth Century when we sorely need a vision of our own peculiar muddle—some accurate reflection of the sty in which we wallow. The anxieties, the nagging fear, the surging dread symptomatic of an ego-centric age are relieved—the pressure is somehow dissipated when we see that others, too, search for meaning in a world that sometimes appears, even to the most secure in faith, magnificently mad.

Much of this tormented writing bursts forth from the fevered works of August Strindberg, who explored the dark world of the mind and the grotesque *danse macabre* of contemporary sex tension.

Strindberg, monstrously unhappy son of a Stockholm barmaid, was begot out of wedlock and always seemed, in the nightmarish misery of his plays, a bastard child to any real joy. He himself fathered a whole group of dramatists whose psychological acuity, whose impressionistic and expressionistic experiment, whose deft use of fragments—half-formed images—have made them uniquely right for the *milieu* of this century and appealing to its dazed inhabitants.

As a matter of simple fact, Strindberg, with Luigi Pirandello, is one of the two major influences in what we call contemporary drama. There is so much in this man that is analogous to the man of today. There is to be found in his work something of modern man's hapless groping for truth and for a vision of God; there is something of his infantile seeking for reassurance in the face of the future's dark; and there is something of the gross sex battle in contemporary culture. All this reflected in Strindberg operates like an intellectual, emotional, spiritual beacon to the playwright who is similarly demon possessed.

One such artist is Ingmar Bergman, Svensk Filmindustri's incandescent author-director whose films have become a source of international conversation and a major point of controversy in the world of cinematic art. Sweeping up prizes at most of the international film competitions, the Bergman name under the directing credit has become a formidable source of film prestige, though the late Carl Anders Dymling, his producer, as well as Bergman himself, agreed that he is relatively "non-commercial."

Films like *Smiles of a Summer Night, The Seventh Seal, Wild Strawberries, Dreams, The Magician,* and *The Virgin Spring,* have become most significant titles among the major accomplishments and attractions of modern screen art. Year after year since approximately 1952, Bergman has produced film classics with almost monotonous regularity. The majority of these have been built with screenplays of his "own devising . . . a bright colored thread sticking out of the dark sack of the unconscious. If I begin to wind up this thread, and I do it carefully, a complete film will emerge." As personal and deeply subjective as these films may seem to their initiator—their creator, the works of Ingmar Bergman are hallmarked with cosmic significance and have become a great source of interest, wonder, and excitement in the world of film criticism today.

Ingmar Bergman is the forty-three-year-old son of a Lutheran minister who admits that his work specifically deals with the problems of religion in contemporary life. He has said of his art:

To me, religious problems are continuously alive. I never cease to concern myself with them; it goes on at every hour of the day. (*Four Screenplays by Ingmar Bergman*).

Questioning, probing, examining, his lens constantly peers at the hard encrustations of surface actions and appearances, seeking to break through the apparent things of everyday existence to the real that underlies them. With meticulous attention to the symbolic significance of sound, of detailed image, of relentless closeup of the human face, and the action of man, Bergman has asked, with the insistence of a fanatic, questions that a preoccupied and bustling world is frantically unwilling to face. The mysteries of birth and death; the paradox of sin and repentance; the miracle of forgiveness; the very existence of a Deity and His attitude toward his creatures, are the sum and substance of Bergman's art.

Ingmar Bergman was born in the university town of Uppsala in 1918. His father became Chaplain to the Royal Court in 1924, so young Bergman moved to Stockholm where he later attended the university as a student of literature and the history of art. After having dropped out of university study to work in the theatre in 1941, he finally came to Svensk Filmindustri as a filmwriter. A year later, his first screenplay, *Torment,* was produced though he did not serve as director. This was but one of four screenplays that Bergman has written and did not direct himself.

It was not until 1956 that Ingmar Bergman loomed large among the major figures of international filmdom. It was that year when his *Smiles of a Summer Night* won a special award at Cannes. From this point on, honors came in quick succession with the 1957 film, *The Seventh Seal,* earning major awards at Cannes, Valladolid, and in the *Grand Prix Internationale de l'Academie du Cinema* in France: with *Brink of Life* securing best director honors at Cannes in 1958; with *Wild Strawberries* garnering five major prizes plus a nomination for an American Academy Award; and with *The Magician* being named "best foreign film of the year" by the Italian film critics while simultaneously walking off with the best directing award at Venice. *The Virgin Spring,* one of the latest film offerings from Bergman's fertile mind to reach the United States, has already won an Academy Award for the best foreign film.

In the introduction to *Four Screenplays of Ingmar Bergman* (New York: Simon and Schuster, 1960), the much-extolled Swede has written that he is vitally concerned with the religious reality in his works. He says that from his earliest childhood as a clergyman's son, he touched upon the world of the spirit. As he puts it:

A child who is born and brought up in a vicarage acquires an early familiarity with life and death behind the scenes. Father performed funerals, marriages, baptisms, gave advice, and prepared sermons. The devil was an early acquaintance and in the child's mind there was a need to personify him.

In a number of his films one can see a great striving to come face to face with not only his personified devil, but with God Himself as well. Through the pulsing imagery of the moving picture camera and through the brilliant series of aural and visual images in which Bergman, the artist, paints, he seeks to achieve a projected image of God through the Divine thread's unravelling in the lives and acts of men. He has been close to achieving this in the near blasphemous and sceptical Christian analogy of *The Face* (*The Magician*) and in the searching morality tale *The Seventh Seal*. *The Virgin Spring*, made in 1959 and brought to this country in 1960, has been thought by many to have represented a positive depiction of God through the panoramic viewing of the whole landscape of lust, rape, murder, revenge, subsequent murder, repentance, forgiveness, and expiation. With the theological orientation of a Tolstoy novel coupled with the simplicity of a Hemingway short story, *The Virgin Spring* depicts the God of the Christians through stumbling humanity created in his image and likeness.

Like so many modern artists, heirs of Strindberg and Pirandello, Bergman shows little faith in the fabric of his work. Faith is lacking and does not even seem to be a sufficient answer to the feverish wants of the Tennessee Williams, the Eugene O'Neills, the Ionescos, the Becketts, and the Genets of the world. Bergman, like all these others, gives no sign that he will be satisfied with faith. As he speaks through his characters in the sombre *The Seventh Seal:*

Knight: I want knowledge, not faith, not suppositions, but knowledge. I want God to stretch out his hand toward me, reveal himself and speak to me.
Death: But if he remains silent.
Knight: I call out to him in the dark, but no one seems to be there.

Death: Perhaps no one is there.
Knight: Then life is an outrageous horror. No one can live in the face of death knowing all is nothingness.

In this film and in the others as well, he manifests a gnawing need for certainty, something that is, we are told, unachievable this side of death. Bergman reiterates again and again a need for certainty and the search for God—a resounding and decisive proof of His existence—goes on in film after film.

In *The Seventh Seal* and the subsequent films of the last five years, this God-seeking turns from a sort of grudging, joy-killing suspicion that God doesn't exist to an overt and searching anxiety; and from a hedonistic agnostic, not terribly concerned about God except to consider Him as a terrible inhibitor of human pleasure, our searcher seems to become an unsated, God-thirsty Deist. An example of this Deistic point of view may be found in *Wild Strawberries* when the two students Professor Borg picks up in his car attempt to settle the question of God's existence with argument and fisticuffs:

Viktor: We swore that we wouldn't discuss God or science on the entire trip. I consider Anders' lyrical outburst as a breach of our agreement.
Sara: Oh, it was beautiful.
Viktor: Besides, I can't see how a modern man can become a minister. Anders isn't a complete idiot.
Anders: Let me tell you that your rationalism is incomprehensible nonsense and you aren't an idiot either.
Viktor: In my opinion the modern—
Anders: In my opinion—
Viktor: In my opinion modern man looks his insignificance straight in the eye and believes in himself and his biological death. Everything else is nonsense.

Like many of the arguments of young men, no conclusion is reached in this verbal battle and, of course, one must be careful not to read the author into either of the characters too readily. There is evidence only that Bergman was conscious of the dilemma and concerned with the problem. He forces no conclusion.

There is considerable Deistic influence in both *Wild Straw-*

berries and *The Seventh Seal* with no divine intervention shown, though the characters question God almost without end and constantly search for Him. Unlike the novels of Bernanos, Mauriac, Graham Greene, and Bergman's own countryman, Sven Stolpe—and all of these men concern themselves with the same subjects that seem lately to obsess them—there is no flowering of God's grace in the world that Bergman creates and shows. Only in *The Magician* is there any manifestation of what might be called grace by any stretch of the imagination, and this, the summons from the king at the last moment, is so clothed in vagueness and misty symbolism that one cannot be sure that it is not merely badly designed *deus ex machina* or a satiric device employed for benefit of cynics as in Brecht's *Threepenny Opera*.

In the films prior to *The Virgin Spring,* grace is not only absent, but denied. In *The Magician* we hear the character Vergerus saying to Doctor Vogler's wife,

But miracles don't happen. It is always the apparatus and the spiel which have to do the work. The clergy have the same experience. God is silent and the people chatter.

This is the Bergman of the 1956–59 period—the creator who looks for God but who cannot find Him. This is reminiscent of a line from another of Strindberg's heirs, Tennessee Williams. Bergman's mention of a "silent God" is mirrored in a speech in Williams' *Sweet Bird of Youth* when the heckler shouts:

I believe that the silence of God, the absolute silence of Him, is a long and awful thing that the whole world is lost because of.

There is despair here and a rebuke that not only echoes the words of Vergerus in *The Magician,* but which brings back the confession scene in *The Seventh Seal* when the knight talks of life's being "a meaningless horror." Williams and Bergman flounder along with the philosophers and scientists seeking the elusive face of truth in a world of chaos and disagreement about man's origin, purpose, and ultimate end.

One can admire the concern of the artist who is "engaged" enough in life to seek its "meaning beyond meaning." In *The*

Seventh Seal, the character Death comments, "Most people never reflect about either death or the futility of life." In this respect, the Bergman preoccupation with eschatological things makes him kindred to those artists of The Age of Faith who saw a death mask behind every grimace, who saw the grave yawning beyond every door, and the blaze of eternity behind every flickering candle. Like the medieval man, Bergman can see humor, horror, and triumph in the apparition of death.

With the release of *The Virgin Spring,* we can no longer tag Bergman as a mere eclectic whose experiments lack pattern and meaning, nor can he be pushed back into the category of blind searchers like Williams and O'Neill, whose devious paths always seem lacking in light. There has been, on the basis of this film's evolution out of the questions posed in those immediately preceding it, a discernible development—a spiritual pattern of search in the work of this man who is concerned solely with the making of films ". . . about conditions, tensions, pictures, rhythms, and characters which are in one way or another important to me." This development indicates that Bergman is in the throes of a genuine search for meaning—he is striving to find the wellsprings of life.

The Virgin Spring marks the first time that Bergman allows God to intervene in the affairs of men. Suddenly the Deistic God, detached from the misery He allows, is transfigured into the God of the Christians—a God of mercy and of grace.

The Virgin Spring recounts a medieval legend of a man who has accepted God and who works for Christianity in those sooty days when Christendom was rising out of the gloomy barbarism of pre-Gothic times. His only child, a shining young virgin, is raped and senselessly killed by two crude goatherds. In his wrath, the father slays them and their innocent child brother who witnessed their deed of lust and blood. And then the father's revengeful spirit is chastened by the sight of the slaughtered boy child and his own bloodied hands become an affront to his Christian heart. Resolving expiation, he confronts his God in a scene of unbelievable conviction and rare power. In this scene the viewer sees something of the spirit Archibald MacLeish might have realized in *J.B.*, but was somehow unable to elicit. Bergman has, whether purposely or not, drawn the heart from the *Book of Job* and has flung it in all its primitive power and truth upon the black and white screen.

For the fact is, Bergman is more truly a poet than many of those who profess to write in the idiom of verse drama. His poetic synthesis of word and image carries a near-Shakespearean splendor and richness, and for one who has said, "I myself have never had any ambition to be an author. I do not want to write novels, short stories, essays, biographies, or even plays for the theatre. I want only to make films . . ." he has really come to an understanding of the complex skein of image, word, and tempo that makes up the tapestry of great art. Bergman has found the vernacular of our age through the incisive images of his darting lens.

There are some who may wish to disqualify the seeming change in Bergman as manifested in *The Virgin Spring* as a mere result of Ulla Isaksson's collaboration. They would have us believe that this influence was the prime cause for creating this film as an affirmation of the regenerative power of God's grace. We choose not to believe this, for Bergman is known for guiding the creations of his hand and mind with an inner force that employs collaborators well, but which keeps all the elements of collaboration in accord with the tyranny of true art. Bergman could not have done this film unless he was in basic accord with its philosophy. Though he may well be using the work as a hypothesis, saying, "Look, my friends, don't you think that this may be the nature of things?" we have no doubt that it is Bergman speaking despite the submission to collaboration. Bergman has collaborated before and speaks with respect of the collaborative nature of artistic endeavor. With or without Isaksson, Per-Anders Fogelström, Herbert Grevenius, or the others with whom he has worked, we can sense that his art has been kept true to the ideals and ideology of the dominant artist who shaped it. This is a man who has turned down Hollywood's money several times for the luxury of maintaining his integrity as an artist.

One can only sit stunned and speechless as this film supports the bursting forth of Divine Power, transmuting the very ravages of deep sin into meaningfulness and an effusion of grace.

The religious fabric of the film, spun from the warp of tangled motives and the woof of twisted malice, is manifested as the protagonist who has been both victim and subsequent victimizer says to God, "I don't understand you! I don't understand you, but still I ask your forgiveness."

Like the father in *The Virgin Spring*, Ingmar Bergman is still trapped in the demoniac night of doubt, but his questions are the right ones that can lead him out of the jungle into the light if he can accept the light, knowing that there is no certainty, only faith, this side of death.

Bergman calls out in one of the confused voices of our age. He calls out loud and clear, "Who is God? Where is He? When will He come?" One who so sincerely and eloquently asks cannot long be denied an answer. In Bergman we meet, in the relatively new art of the screen, one who like Sophocles and Shakespeare seeks the ends of art in the beginnings of eternity.

In the American theatre we can find a striking parallel to Bergman in our own much-extolled Eugene O'Neill. In O'Neill we find, and it is no surprise, a playwright who not only acknowledges a debt to a Scandinavian playwright, Strindberg, but one whose plays have found enduring fame in Sweden, the homeland of his inspiration.

Eugene Gladstone O'Neill was once quoted as saying:

There can be no such thing as an ivory tower for a playwright. He either lives in the theatre o fhis time or he never lives at all. (*The Curse of the Misbegotten*).

O'Neill not only practiced what he preached, dwelling on his own troubled age, but his own life reflected something of the despairing confusion of our times in a microcosm of grief and loneliness.

O'Neill recognized that the contemporary age is an ego-centric one. Whereas medieval man lived in a Christo-centric era with all things centered about the altar; the Athenian lived in a socio-centric society with all things ordered around the state—the *polis;* and the Renaissance man dwelt in a world fascinated and revolving about the discoveries of humanism —a homo-centric age we might call it; we of the Twentieth Century dance about ourselves—the great "I"—like some spiritual maypole thrust up in great pride. O'Neill felt this egocentricity and was a part of it, and he sought to escape its intrinsic loneliness by setting out in search for the elemental force behind what seems a cold, cruel world. Not satisfied with his contacts with fellow man, the obsessed O'Neill sought the eternal, the cosmic, the unchanged and unchanging, only to become a victim of the modern world himself —to become trapped in its paucity of spiritual imagination.

Like most of us living today, he found distasteful the stiff formulas of Victorian ethics which have somehow percolated into Christian thought today. Seeking a broader, bigger arena for living and a God great enough to live for, O'Neill was gulled by the effete mast the Victorians had erected before the terrible God of Mount Sinai and seeking beyond and elsewhere he found only the terrible shadows of faith, which is, in the words of the stirring Australian Catholic novelist, Morris West, "the antechamber to revelation." And lacking faith he thought God dead, so he turned to the green-faced little gods man builds himself when he cannot reach the real one.

With his own castaway, if somewhat incomplete, concept of Catholicism (underlining guilt, cosmic consciousness, and a certain Jansenistic revulsion from things of the flesh which rode his spirit hard) his plays teetered on the brink of the infinite. However, only once did he really start to slide over the edge, with *Days Without End,* only to betray his intention with his all too characteristic weakness of technique. The magnificence of his themes and the theatrical soundness of his work is beyond question but there were times—and very often too—that O'Neill's inability to "write"—dialogue, character, etc.—caught up with him and betrayed him badly. On a less superficial level, O'Neill was restrained from the abyss of God because he knew nothing of mercy and grace. Because, touched by modern rationalism, O'Neill sought answers where there are only mysteries, he was frustrated in his quest for God. From such a chase, one in which answers and formulae are demanded this side of death, only disillusion can result.

Filled with the spirit of Nietzche, Schopenhauer, and Freud, and writing in the artistic heritage of Strindberg, O'Neill's universe is a black one—a place in torment and terror. Out of thirty-seven plays, for instance, there are only five free from murder, suicide, violent death, or insanity. He treats of incest, rape, murder, suicide, and the more violent forms of psychosis. He dwells again and again upon the capital sins and even pushes the limits of human endurance with such vices as abortion and cannibalism. He ends one play (*Dynamo*) with a man hurling himself as a human sacrifice into an electrical dynamo where his dying screams are drowned out by the impersonal hum of machinery, and yet, after reading several of his works, Sister Mary Madeleva, poetess and educator, could say:

I'm sure Eugene O'Neill was profoundly Catholic in mind and in heart. They (*Long Day's Journey Into Night* and *Days Without End*) are parts of the same story of an extraordinary soul almost childlike in its attempts to spell God with the wrong blocks. (*The Curse of the Misbegotten*).

There is less childhood in O'Neill, however, than there is adult madness, for there is a quality in his work that suggests a man trying to scream down a whirlwind. Dion-Anthony, the autobiographical character, half Dionysius and half St. Anthony of the Desert, says in *The Great God Brown*:

"I've loved, lusted, won and lost, sung and wept."

And so he had, in a life and art that was vivid, restless, excited, terrible, and at bottom, tragic.

O'Neill, like his idol, Strindberg, wrote of the Passion of man. Not passion in the vernacular corruption of the word, but passion far closer to the basic definition of the word— something endured—something *done to* man—not man *doing*, but man the victim.

This is not to suggest that O'Neill is a determinist on the order of Stephen Crane and Frank Norris, or farther afield, Zola in France, for in substituting Freud for Christ or at least for "the old Gods" of the Greeks, he still allows man the stature of will-power. O'Neill's characters maintain their right to choose. It is not man bereft of choice that he gives us, but man challenged and challenging—looking heavenward—outward from his soul with a human dare to cast out into the cosmos. Unlike the heroes (such as they are) of determinism, O'Neill's figures present and preserve dignity—something of the essential nature of man.

O'Neill's pessimism is clearly related to that of Strindberg and is similarly a product of an apparently unhappy life. A sensate, driving nature, shackled to a disjointed childhood as son of a frustrated actor whose very success as The Count of Monte Cristo conspired to constrain him and poison his family. O'Neill could not accommodate himself to school or to any other so called "steady" endeavor. His restlessness drove him to move from place to place, from job to job, from experience to experience. From place to place he wandered, seeking his Grail, alternately exhilarated and despairing.

Chapter Six

From Pilate's Chair

"What is Truth?"

I'M NOT as yet sure that I know what the *avant garde* theatre really is. I'm not sure that anyone does. We hear a great deal about it. The news magazines play it up with delightful pictures of people in exotic masks, girls with horsetails and sexy dance tights, musclemen making love to grandmothers, and little men peeping out from under trash can lids. They talk about the old Floogle Street routine of the burlesque circuit and they have a grand time kidding titles like *On The Runway of Life You Never Know What's Coming Off Next.* It's all rather fascinating and because it's a bit more comprehensible than junk art and a trifle more *chic* than folk music, people have become captivated by the whole thing. As a matter of fact, the *avant garde* theatre has almost completely displaced "The Method" as a topic of polite controversy for people buzzing about the theatre.

The critics, too, are fascinated. At first they ignored the whole thing, hoping it would go away. Then as the public clamor increased, the critics, afraid to be called ignorant by the sports car set who frequent the *avant garde* playhouses, went along for laughs. Some were impressed. Others *said* they were impressed. Some didn't understand but they said they were impressed too.

It also gives them marvellous opportunities to make comparisons, filled as it is with tag lines from here and there, odd terms, and memorable images, and of course such comparisons are often the critic's refuge. When he can think of nothing else to say, he makes comparisons. It's rather fun, and if it isn't really criticism, it's at least the sign of an alert mind and a retentive memory.

A few years back, William Saroyan, whose plays would likely be considered *avant garde* if they weren't already thought *passé*, published a sort of *apologia*—a kind of justification for the theatre of the *avant garde*. In this short piece which prefaced two Ionesco plays in a national theatre magazine, Saroyan spoke reverently of the bravery of the *avant*

67

gardists and of the fact that he considers today's *avant garde* as the respectable, first-class drama of tomorrow, just as yesterday's experimentalists became the major playwrights of our times.

It isn't surprising that Saroyan should speak this way, for throughout his whole career to date, he himself attempted to be as experimental and shockingly offbeat as possible. Unlike the *avant gardists* of today, Saroyan does betray a genuine understanding of the human heart—of human dream and aspiration. Nevertheless, like them—the Ionescos, the Becketts, and the Albees—he did not in any sense stand by conventional forms or attitudes. It's still questionable as to how much of this was a matter of artistic intent and how much was merely a matter of not learning the rudiments of playwriting form. Still, it is not surprising that we find Saroyan tooting a horn for the *avant garde,* for he seems to feel, the marvellous sentimentalist, like an older brother to those who write under its flashy banner.

His premise that yesterday's experimenters become today's greats is a rather dubious proposition. It's worth noting that neither Sophocles, Lope de Vega, Shakespeare, Marlowe, Corneille, Racine, or Molière was a *real* innovator. To be sure, most of these men did make interesting and occasionally significant contributions in technique or subject matter to the theatre of their age, but most of all they traded on their brilliance as followers of a dramatic mode already established. Their *real* contribution was in bringing the experiments of Aeschylus and his anonymous predecessors, de Rueda, Heywood, Jodelle and all the other early writers of their trspective ages to a point of artistic wholeness—theatrical maturity. History proves that the *avant gardist* is a sacrificial goat, rarely writing well himself, but allowing bigger and better artists to walk over him on their way to immortality. If the *avant garde* of today serves such a function we can rejoice to put up with their outrages.

It would seem, however, that the *avant garde* theatre takes itself somewhat more seriously. They are not content as were the dramaturgical trailblazers of antiquity to come up with brand new techniques of the same old drama—seeking to put the "real" onstage—but they would blast *all* tradition to one side, even denying that there is a "real" to be gotten at, in their brash and self-confident efforts to "clean up the theatre."

There's no question in anyone's mind that our theatre today couldn't be immensely improved. It could do vastly better than it's doing at the present time. Though we haven't yet fully cornered the market on banality, we seem to be getting there fast and only rarely does our contemporary theatre come up with something genuine, human, and "real." It's rather to be expected that there will be, in periods of theatrical weakness, groups of sincere artists trying, by almost any conceivable method, to turn a cheap theatre back into worthier channels. This is essentially what the *avant gardist* is trying to do and in the very lack of satisfaction in our current theatre we find the reason why certain critics and certain audiences are willing to support him. For the impatient, any change must be a good change.

Perhaps the most distressing thing about the *avant garde* theatre is that its proponents do not seem so much intent on giving us a new theatre as they do in giving us a new moral code, a new theology, and a completely new synthesis of knowledge. I suppose this would be very well and good, after a fashion, if we'd really tried the moral code, the theology, and the human knowledge we already have and had found them wanting. Gilbert Chesterton once said, with a note of seriousness, too, I fancy, that Christianity's biggest problem was that it has never been really tried out. He may have something, and it is precisely in these terms that we may meet the assault of the *avant gardists*.

Keeping in step with the great critic Nathan's statement that a drama critic without prejudices is like a general who refuses to take human life, I here assert that I am wholly prejudiced in favor of man, his essential human nature, and in the values—the dramatic values—that stem from his nature. We go to the theatre to see man confronting himself. We go to witness a rational, free-willed creature operating in a staggering, mysterious, at times cruel and perverse, but always grandly wonderful, universe. We go to hear impelling and beautiful words and to be excited and thrilled by the proximate evidence of truth and beauty that good theatre can give.

We don't really go to see psychological or sociological case histories. For example, *Krapp's Last Tape* gives a remarkable case study of a senile man who, upon listening to tape recordings made in his youth, surrenders hope and sinks into lethargic despair; Edward Albee's much-touted *The Zoo Story* tells of a lonely neurotic who confronts the citizen of today's middle class in the park and succeeds after a long unhappy conversation in having the prim and proper fellow put an end to his unhappy life; Jean Genet's *The Balcony* asks Pilate's great question in terms of unspeakable blasphemies, genuine pornography, and a whole skein of psychological aberrations; and the plays of Eugene Ionesco, with all their bizarre theatricality, are comments on the mind—the sadly disoriented mind—of modern man. Perhaps these questions, these pressing questions, merit exploration. Since Pontius Pilate flicked his wet fingers in the face of Christ, we have been asking the question, "What is truth?"

Recently, to my surprise—or maybe it was shock—a Catholic college professor said to me, in all seriousness, that a Roman Catholic cannot really be a creative artist. He said that an artist asks questions and for a Catholic, all essential, really basic questions are answered in the Baltimore Catechism. He claimed that the questioning of serious art implies a lack of faith.

There was no question about his sincerity, just as there's no question about the sincerity of millions of devout Christians, Catholics and non-Catholics, who believe this. He was utterly convinced that art was, for these reasons, completely unnecessary for a true Catholic individual, if not absolutely wrong. Many people today act on the basis that art is unnecessary, but one wonders how many of those so concerned really feel as they imply. In this man's case, all one can do is admire his faith and shudder at his rigidity.

By way of refuting his thesis we can point to human love in order to find a workable analogy. Needless to say, when one deeply loves another person and knows that his love is returned, it is still wholesomely reassuring to hear the words "I love you," from time to time. It in no way implies a lack of confidence in the bond of love or the contract of matrimony when the wife asks her beloved husband, "Do you love me? Tell me."

Similarly, there are times when we feel it necessary to whistle in the face of eternity. There are times when life becomes so bewildering, so staggering, so lacking in sense and logic, those untrustworthy guides, that we find it necessary to seek assurance—to gain some glimpse of order in the universe— the universe which looks like whirling chaos every once in a while. Sometimes, regardless of faith, it is inevitable that the question of Pilate goes whizzing through our consciousness and we seek to be reassured. "Show us ourselves and our lives," we cry to the artist. "Show us man and make us happy to be men—or at least, help us be reconciled to our lot!"

But one must wonder at the search afforded us through the *avant garde* theatre. Is it *really* a help to us? Does it *really* serve to recreate us—to enhance our lives—to "lift us up and outside ourselves"? One fears that it is more fad than fashion and more fashion than philosophy. We go to the *avant garde* cupboard like Mother Hubbard's starving dog and find it terribly, terribly bare though they lead us to believe that it is full. Like sophomores who write for college literary magazines and make obscurity and negation their stock in trade, the *avant garde* dramatists have found that a certain audience, a peculiar minority, is attracted by the grotesqueries of psychosis, irrationality, and wonderfully theatrical perversion. Styling themselves as experimentalists these men—Albee, Beckett, Genet, Gelber and others—are like so many boys with chemistry sets, tossing all sorts of materials into their test tubes, hoping against hope it will at least bubble or cause a minor explosion.

Working with shock and a disconnected sort of irrationality, these men find that it isn't strictly necessary to write a good play in order to achieve success in the modern theatre. It's merely sufficient to write something so shockingly incomprehensible or blatantly symbolic that it violates every canon in the whole artistic tradition and you'll find a certain group ready to go along. With a kind of virtuoso "nuttiness" they expand medical histories and social treatises, throw conventional technique out the window, adopt some of the more discredited devices of Constructivism, and make a completely new and arbitrary set of rules known only to themselves. Once having done this, they sit back, expecting to be venerated as the precursors of the new and "live" theatre. It's rather like playing a new game with the fellow who made it up. Whenever he wins a trick against you he justifies it with a new rule—a rule he's probably just made up for the occasion. When writing a play and doing it for a normal audience one should give the audience some idea of what game is being played and some rudimentary idea of what the rules will be. This is the only genuinely effective way in which you can communicate to them.

The *avant gardists* seem to feel that in a disjointed century, where sense and sensibility are beaten down by all sorts of evils and absurdities, their plays must follow suit and become as unfathomable as the times. Instead of bringing order to chaos, rationality to confusion, lucidity to psychosis, they merely bring more coal to Newcastle, aggravate the whole sorry situation and make the staggering world an even noisier, more dangerous Bedlam than it is.

There's no question but that man has cast away a good deal of his dignity. In this society in which we claw for survival, man has degraded and cheapened himself. The examples are all around us. It's nothing terribly surprising. History shows us that man does this every now and then. However, the norm is still there and man still bears, whether he knows it or not, somewhere in the cruciform lump of flesh he appears to be, an unquenchable innate dignity. The drama's traditional, historic role has been to affirm and explore this innate dignity. We can have no patience for a theatre which denies this dignity and sulks in hideous despair, refusing to go out and search for light and truth.

The most talked about *avant gardist* of them all seems to be Rumanian-born, French playwright, Eugene Ionesco. Ionesco, despite being at the root of this *avant garde* thing and using the most startling images of them all, is the most likely playwright of the whole pack.

Following very much in the footsteps of Franz Kafka, Ionesco uses monstrous images to point up and question the manners and ideals of today. The inanities of everyday conversation are satirized in *The Bald Soprano*, the egotistical demands of modern educators are scored in *The Lesson*, the modern sin of conformism is brilliantly indicted in *Rhinocerus*. These are things that may very well be said by the dramatist of today, but one questions, in the case of *The Bald Soprano*, whether the theatre should waste her time with three quarters of an hour of inane conversation gleaned from a French grammar, just to manifest the boring repetitiveness of modern social intercourse. One wonders! It's all very brilliant the first time or two around.

There seems little doubt that Ionesco can write. *Rhinocerus* is a rather fine play and despite the unorthodox approach it involves, it makes its points validly and dramatically. Unlike some of the shorter plays it does not lose its audience in a welter of subjective symbols.

Samuel Beckett, also considered a high priest of the movement (if this is a proper term for it), has gained a great deal of attention for the objectives and methods of *avant gardism*, though we may legitimately question just how *avant* this Joycean writer really is. More Joyce than Kafka, he doesn't seem to be a specie of the same genus that includes Ionesco.

Philosophically, Beckett seems to hold a rather futile position and the oft-used justification for *avant gardism*, that they are seeking to inject purpose into a bankrupt society, doesn't seem at all applicable to his work. Beckett stands for a position of hopelessness—that nothing really can be done and that we must all fall into the grave unfulfilled. His *Waiting For Godot*, with its pseudo-mysterious obviousness, showed us a completely nihilistic point of view. In *Endgame*, the much wondered-at significance of people living in trash cans seems brutally obvious and as with all Becket's writing, the only real cure for life seems to be death as quickly served as possible.

Jean Genet's theatre, ritualistic and wild, seems perhaps most clearly in search of truth, but seems most heavily smeared with the offal of irrelevancy. *The Balcony*, one of his most talked about plays, seems a reasonably accurate reiteration of the "What is truth?" theme, though in the erotic framework of its setting Genet seems to have betrayed his own basic purpose by making it so pornographically diverting that one can scarcely see the real spine of the work under the whorehouse analogy that dominates it.

Genet writes with boldness and verve. Genet conjures up brutally arresting images. Genet has an ability to shock that would likely gratify Antonin Artaud, the fascinating and half mad advocate of shock in the theatre, but since when do these off-beat gifts make a significant dramatist?

Here in the United States, the pattern for *avant garde* theatre seems to have been one of steady gain. Largely through the works of Ionesco, Beckett, and Genet in translation, and through the native attempts of Albee, Gelber, and Kopit, the *avant garde* has built up a strong beachhead off-Broadway and in the columns of a number of highly respectable critics.

It is incredible to consider that on the basis of four plays, one little more than a fragment, Edward Albee, the *enfant terrible* of America's *avant garde,* is being seriously considered in many quarters as a genuinely important playwright. The same critics and theorists who deny Thornton Wilder his legitimate right to be called a great playwright because he has written so little are ready to canonize young Albee as the greatest thing in modern drama.

This neatly tailored young man, who sounds quite rational and even personable, writes like a bomb-carrying anarchist. Without benefit of beret and red armband he seems to be principal among the new iconoclasts in our theatre. This group, claiming some inspiration from Ionesco, causing many a theatre-goer to shake his head in helpless bewilderment, seek, it seems, to shake the contemporary theatre to its roots, to put mystery back on a stage that has become enamored of fact and completely captivated by obvious *formulae*—a theatre which to them has become ossified.

The idea, on the surface, sounds quite commendable. Our American theatre has certainly been guilty of a narcissism that has disgusted many of its patrons and practitioners. Inbred, obsessed with its own fancied significance, prudently unoriginal and technique-ridden, it is overdue for the guillotine of meaningful revolt.

There is little doubt that the American theatre needs change and there's little doubt that such change will be forthcoming. There is, though, a valid question as to whether that change need be revolutionary in nature. There are times when revolution is needed. There are times when, in violence, the old order must be swept away—obliterated to make way for the new. But then, we mustn't be too precipitous in praising just *any* change, for the theatre is the art of man, the art through which he most triumphantly asserts his humanity, his rationality, his glorious birthright of free will, and the wondrous circumstances of his creation. The *avant gardist,* in his eagerness for change, in his fever for the joyous madness of demolition, does not offer this. He does not promise us that any such great theatre will arise from the ashes of the old. Instead he offers a collage of marginal comprehensibility, a collection of carefully collated contemporary inanities, devoid of order or any hint that beyond mystery's dark veil an unchanging truth may lie hidden. He offers only incongruity, the perverse and bizarre, and the unexpected. He offers no hint of a criteria for normalcy.

The unexpected is of minimal value in the theatre. The great audiences of antiquity—Shakespeare's, Corneille's, Lope de Vega's and that of the Greeks—witnessed spectacles that were partly or wholly familiar to them. They watched and heard old stories whose very familiarity made them intensely comprehensible and gave the playwright, when he became intent on communicating a theme, an ideal vehicle upon which to bear it.

In contrast, the *avant garde* has all but abandoned normal communication. They have dragged obscurity, shock, and surprise into "the temple of evidence."

Undoubtedly the *avant gardist,* and Albee here provides a fortunate case in point, has an axe to grind. He is original— terrifically original—and in his originality, extreme as it may often be, lies his strength. Nevertheless, it is difficult to peer through the smokescreen of paradox to see whether or not he really has something to say. In the theatre the audience doesn't *bother* to comprehend unless the playwright, within the generally accepted and known conventions of the stage, says what he has to say in a reasonably overt manner. No audience can sit happily guessing as to what the playwright means. They demand to know exactly what the playwright is driving at. They demand this and when they don't get it they become sullen, bored, restless, and the magical commerce of the play is lost.

Peculiarly enough, the *avant gardist* talks about man's failure to communicate. He notes the lack of love and understanding in the world and he stands up and howls dismally that men are horrible walled islands shut up within themselves, fated never to break loose from their bleak isolation. The terrible pair in *The Zoo Story* talking *at* each other instead of *with* each other, never genuinely touching each other in communication, likely embody this point of view as clearly as anything Albee has written, though Ionesco has managed it time and time again. In the tradition of Kafka, the *avant garde* playwright shows us how horrible our isolation is. Again we cannot indict him for speaking thus, for this is a real terror and no meaningless bogey.

The *avant gardist* despairs of the modern theatre's technique and it is at this point we can scream derision at the precocious band who would level our theatre and render it a grotesque playground of their own devising. One needn't argue with their position that our modern world is a piteous place, constipated with egocentricity and bilious with smugness. We can accept this analysis and we can cheer any sincere and well-chosen efforts taken to better it. We *can* question the *means*, however, and it is in the means that the commendable objectives of some of the *avant gardists* (like Albee who does not appear a nihilist) are tragically betrayed.

In these cases, and let's use Albee for an example, we can note that he neither lectures interestingly like Brecht, delights and outrages like Shaw, nor sings like O'Casey as he slings his thunderbolts into the world's teeth. He fails dismally in getting his audiences up and outside themselves. He only slaps them back into the lonely cell of ego where they must dwell unfulfilled and in spineless terror. Albee is too busy indulging in private ironies to share with the humble generosity that is inevitably present in an artist who is earnest and true.

The stage deals in symbols and conventions. It must give freely of itself in the beautiful social intercourse of the play, that thrilling transfer of thought, emotion, and even on rare occasions, spirit. Albee's theatre gives nothing. It seeks attention in return for the dry crust of a spurious mystery. A cocatenation of the same *non sequiturs* and banalities one hears on the street are poor payment indeed for those who come to the theatre.

One must not infer, in all of this, that theatrical experimentalism is to be questioned. Only through reasonable experimentation, with the erosive testing of ideas and execution in the acid-filled retort of performance and rehearsal and subsequent criticism, through the labor pains of the innovator who has given birth to the new idea and ideal, can the old theatre regenerate itself. It is only when the whelp runs in, fangs bared, with no real knowledge of or regard for the rules of the house, that those not afraid to be called cowards or louts must defend the canons of art.

There is a relevant point in the classic fairy-tale, *The Emperor's New Clothes,* in which everyone fears to cry out the obvious truth that the Emperor is bare. Everyone fears to be called stupid for failing to see the clothes which are, as a matter of fact, not there. This damnable fear is ever the protection of the faddist.

Edward Albee, brash young novice, has torn off the white veil of humility and is confidently belching in the sanctuary of art. He writes for the narrow audience, an audience far removed from the broad pastures of grassroots participation where great plays are grown. His *Zoo Story,* following the hysterical indictments of conformity and self-isolation contributed by some of the European *avant gardists,* really paves the way for a new and insidious kind of conformism—one in which personal responsibility and the inexorable obligations occasioned by man's social nature are trampled under by the *new* herd.

The type of freedom extolled in *The Zoo Story* (and it's the same in such dismal trash as Lonny Chapman's *Cry of the Raindrop* and in the brief Broadway appearance of Arthur Laurent's *Invitation to a March*) is a perverted concept and Albee manifests with these others a frightening confusion

77

between freedom *for* principle as opposed to freedom *as* principle. The difference is crucial and marks the boundary line where responsible human liberty leaves off and the tyranny of license begins. Albee, along with the others, recognizes no such distinction and would likely ridicule the idea that "The truth will make you free."

The Death of Bessie Smith provides us with the sight of another level of Albee's mendacity. This short play, set in a small hospital of the American South, seems a murky visitation to a world of abnormality—a hooded world of psychological aberration where man's motives are never clear and clean, but ever murky, never stemming from rationality, but from a sort of blind impulse. This sort of treatment vitiates the purpose of drama which involves the operation of the volitional man in a rational framework of purpose. All the play manifests is some talent for aping down-to-earth, repetitive dialogue true to his setting. A tape recorder can do nearly as much. Poor Bessie, planted anonymously in a Philadelphia grave, is ignored, despite the play's promising title.

The Sandbox, which is rather misleadingly described as a *play* in one scene, reaches new heights in obscurity with a middle-aged couple popping a senile granny into a child's sandbox at the shore. The old woman finds herself mightily attracted to the Angel of Death disguised as a muscle-bound beach boy. After some nearly incoherent theatrical tradespoofs in which the scene itself is mocked, the woman apparently dies, though it's difficult to be sure. Walter Kerr has referred to this piece as a "single, oddly satisfying sigh" and given it some cautious praise, seeming to approve Albee's clever impudence. One suspects, however, that in making the evaluation, Kerr is speaking as much from the ranks of theatre buffs who can enjoy a joke now and then as he is for the critical fraternity. Kerr, something of a playwright himself, is likely enamored of the accidentals of *The Sandbox* with its waspishly clever dialogue and its fey kidding of convention. It is not, however, a credible play, nor even a well conceived vignette.

There is no question that the tongues of our world today speak in a variety of accents. Like the hosts at the foot of

Babel tower, we still mill about in disunity and there is room —no doubt for it—for disparate opinions and ideologies. It is regrettable, however, to find those whose minds are supposed to be relatively clear, those to whom the world so often listens, caught in a confusion far worse than that of the average man. It is distressing to find them in possession of but a tiny spark of truth they will not even share at the risk of surrendering their own self-adulation. Obscurity makes a remarkably good hiding place for those with minimal talents. The *avant gardist* too often seems a foul-mouthed child who refuses to give up his toys and though his mind may have achieved some maturity, he still insists on speaking in the disjointed utterances of the playroom floor.

Some time ago, Albee, as a self-appointed spokesman for off-Broadway and the theatre of *avant gardism,* spoke before a curious audience in a crowded upstairs room at Philadelphia's Art Alliance. Prefacing the bitter discourse with his usual remarks about having written a sex farce at twelve— a full length sex farce, mind you—he sailed into a fierce diatribe on the Broadway theatre in which he repeatedly compared it to "a stinking carcass—a heap of rotting offal." After demolishing it thoroughly, he launched into a wildly romantic testimonial to what he described as "that fair-faced child"— the theatre of off-Broadway.

When in the subsequent question and answer period he was queried as to why his adored off-Broadway theatre (specifically that part of it devoted to *avant garde* works) insists on doing precisely that for which he sneers at Broadway— writing miniscule characters, vastly smaller than life—he answered with the words, "Marx and Freud." At this point with great tenacity he hewed to the point and despite the urging of a group of genuinely irate listeners, he refused to explicate further on this somewhat enigmatic answer. That which he might well have contributed by pursuing further his own answer, evasive as it may have been, he pointedly passed by.

It is a sad thing to see a young man—even one as intellectually complacent and self satisfied as Albee appears to be— given such adulation so early. Adulation that allows him to evade, even within himself, the problem of self-justification. Many a potential talent has been ruined by the flush of early success, and though to this date Albee has achieved only limited production in small theatres and under one management, he has been widely lionized as the champion of the new stage form, as the beardless young prophet who will deliver our theatre from the old nasty ways.

Perhaps if he takes the trouble to master his craft, if he builds endurance for his short-winded muse, if he correlates his natural ear for modern speech to something rational and truly dramatic, he will in time become a playwright to reckon with. He may even become the theatrical Messias for which the American theatre stands waiting.

This, of course, presumes that all these things can be done before Arthur Kopit, eminent young author of *Oh Dad, Poor Dad, Mamma's Hung You in the Closet and I'm Feeling So Sad* and *On The Runway of Life You Never Know What's Coming Off Next*, captivates the sports car set, and poor Albee becomes a has-been before he reaches his artistic puberty. Otherwise he may be brushed off like so many other fleas and gnats from the great body of our theatre that seems somehow to survive despite the minor irritations that it suffers from time to time.

Chapter Seven

The Bloodshot World

Misanthropy in the Modern Theatre

THE most disturbing thing about the Rabelaisian denunciations of Brendan Behan, as he squints at us through bloodshot eyes, is that much of what he says is true. We dwell in a bawdy-house of our own making—a society full of cacophony and disputation—hypocrisy and cant. Though the ideals and high purposes of a Christian life are as valid as they were in the days when Christ walked the earth, our execution of them might utterly destroy the patience of anything less than Divinity.

Brendan Behan, born in the erupting Dublin of 1923, is a disturbed child of the modern world. Taking up the bomb as a way of life in his thirteenth year, Behan spent most of his life popping in and out of jail like a jack-in-the-box, meanwhile writing and buzzing about like an enraged hornet and getting as marked a reaction from the world he stung. Only in the relatively mellow period of his thirty-ninth year has he become sedate enough to savor the life of the literary man.

Popularly known to the American public for his boozy ramblings in theatres where his plays are done and through his comparatively mild philosophizing on television's "The Jack Paar Show," Behan has become known as a sort of Gaelic clown-prince, a rambling ambassador of the new Irish-Bohemianism. Nothing could be farther from the truth.

In his autobiographical *The Borstal Boy* and in his two rather dissimilar plays, *The Quare Fellow* and *The Hostage*, Behan has set a good many tongues wagging with the violent ribaldry of his pen. His works are stuffed with four-letter words, blasphemy, blatant irreverence, and a gift for controversial statement, along with an undeniable poetic sense.

People who witness the play, *The Hostage*, laugh till they cry, scream to high heaven later that the play should be shut down by the law, and then live to be haunted by the violent crudeness of Behan's denunciations and, of course, their relevance. Behan is a social critic who uses blasphemy for a purpose, a polemicist with a bag full of bombs. This is hardly surprising from a man who carried cordite and TNT as the playthings of puberty.

Though he has been frequently attacked on artistic grounds after the moralists have spent themselves in righteous indignation, Behan is remarkably valid as an artist. Chalking obscenities on the outhouse wall of the world—and the theatre does provide the world with such a facility—Behan represents a literal sort of neo-classicism in which lives the Aristotelian analogy, crude as it is, that the theatre is a place of emotional defecation. However, rather than producing catharsis, Behan seems to indulge in it himself.

Behan is a nostalgic, sentimental man and surely this trait cannot be a surprise in any Irishman. The two great expatriates, Joyce and O'Casey, though far from O'Connell Street and the River Liffey, always betrayed a sad longing for the paths of their youth. Behan, who still walks the streets of his native city between visits to pub, "pokey," and the United States, shows a similar nostalgia for the innocence of youth— for the religious warmth of boyhood.

In *The Borstal Boy* he speaks in a surprisingly sentimental way of serving Mass in an English reform school. He talks of kneeling on the altar steps beside an English Catholic lad from the outside,

. . . murmuring the responses and thinking of my mother singing "In that dread hour when on my bed I'm lying," while she rubbed hell out of the washboard, and of my grandmother, snaking a pinch of snuff to her nostril during the sermon in Gardiner Street, and of old Sister Monica, telling us to go asleep with our arms folded so that if we died during the night, we'd have a cross on us. I forgot everything but what I was doing. *Introibo ad altare Dei. Ad Deum Qui laetificat juventutem meam.*

In this reverie amidst exile, despite Behan's excommunication as a member of the Irish Republican Army, and despite the brutalizing experience of reform school and prison, we see the petulant idealist who stands shaking his fist at God and country for not allowing him a better world.

We also see something of his attitude toward the Church as an open anti-clerical. In the violent interview described when the Borstal boy met the hard-hearted Father Lane, we see the sad human toll exacted by priestly uncharity, that rare and hurtful thing. The lonesome boy, hoping for warm priestly help, reacts violently to the cold harshness of the chaplain and as a mere boy finds himself incapable of seeing beyond the man and the place and the time. His reaction is naive and childish, but understandable in one young, alone, and for all his crust of defiance, afraid.

It is in this violent naïvete, so characteristic of rebellious children, that Behan's weakness lies, for with all his latent idealism, one can scarcely canonize petulance, and impatience is not to be confused with the theological virtue of hope.

The Hostage, the core offering of Behan's formal blasphemy, is an indictment of law, religion, home, country, human decency, art, and even death—things that Behan, like all men, loves or fears and at the very least, respects. Despite a little *apologia* printed in the program which denies that he reverences anything other than that which ". . . makes the roads safer, the beer stronger, or the old men and women warmer in the winter and happier in the summer." Behan shows himself the discountenanced dreamer, the irritated idealist, in the very fervor of the indictments. We are introduced to a world of tarts, pimps, and homosexuals where there is, under the clever banter and song, a bitter mourning for lost innocence.

Strung on a flimsy thread of a plot, the characters philosophize, complain, yell at each other, and do self-consciously outrageous things to the utter, if somewhat carefully concealed, delight of the audience. It is a funny play, but in the broader aspects of its form, it's the humor of a puny ant shaking his insect fist at the man who stands over him with upraised and threatening foot. The ant cries out, "I'm not going to believe in you—I'll call you names! See how you like that!"

He rebels at everything. Not satisfied with a bevy of outrageous "queers," he dubs one of them Princess Grace. He has a whopping good time at the expense of the Irish clergy and while he's a bit less sly about it than James Joyce, he's no less outspoken. Even the theatre, here his chosen medium of expression, is given no quarter, for he continually spoofs the form and causes theatre buffs to snort, "This isn't a play.

It's a vaudeville sketch or burlesque!" There's really an element of truth in this, of course, for the players sing, dance, and engage in burlesque roughhouse.

Death, too, is brazenly funned at, but the jubilant jangling of "the bells of hell" strikes a note of falseness and in the shrill rejection of the young soldier's death at the final curtain —as he clambers to his feet to trill saucily at the audience, "The bells of hell go ting-a-ling-a-ling for *you* and not for me"—one can see a hollow, schoolyard type of defiance flaunted in the face of the grim angel, Sariel. It is a defiance shown hollow in making the comparison with *The Quare Fellow*, an earlier Behan play. In that work, *jongleur* Behan plays "The Minstrel Boy" on a muted horn and there he shows a true dread of that day of wrath we all face.

The Quare Fellow, which at times plays more like a tract than a play, is a rather morbid depiction of the effects of an execution upon the inhabitants of a prison—convicts and guards alike. Illuminated only occasionally by flashes of gallows-humor and now and then by vivid insights of the lonely and denuded state of men in jail, *The Quare Fellow* is more a self-pitying pamphlet than a play.

To be sure there is validity in Behan's discussion of capital punishment, for he seems to feel with John Donne and Walt Whitman that all men are diminished by the extinction of a human life—a single human life. The brutalization of the inflictors of such punishment and the welling guilt felt by those who must commit bureaucratic assassination makes *The Quare Fellow* an arresting piece of human psychology and an interesting sociological treatise, if something way short of genuinely good drama.

Behan's sympathy for his fellow creature is immense. In all his work there seems to be a true love for the harlot, the coward, the old, and the stupid. There is a love for the halt and the blind and the demented, and while he laughs and causes us to laugh at them, it is the laughter of a brother— the bitterness never as deep as the sympathy—the real compassion. Even the British are treated with love and understanding; a bit difficult to understand coming from a veteran I.R.A. bomber.

Behan's language is interesting. He gives definite signs of being well-versed in Ireland's literary traditions. There's a Joycean quality in much of what he writes as he juxtaposes incredibly shocking terms, the jargon of Catholic philosophy, and patches of lyric beauty. The combination is extremely well-suited to the theatre. There is an essential conflict— an intrinsic inner tension—set up within the language itself that seems almost to compensate for the relative *stasis* of his plotting.

As for speech patterns in the dialogue, both in the plays and the autobiographical work, there is rather to be expected evidence that his ear is good for both the patterns of Irish talk and that of Britain in its several dialects. There is great credibility too in the raw, profane talk of gaol.

In the freedom of Behan's language there is further emphasis given to the fact that he stands forth with great ardor for the freedom of the human spirit. He is not likely as anarchistic a thinker as he sometimes suggests himself to be, for surely one would expect a man who has spent more than seven of his thirty-eight years in prison to be antagonistic to law in any form and to those who enforce it. We can suppose, nevertheless, that this seeming anarchy is more a matter of reflex than genuine conviction.

There are those amongst us who have no patience for Behan and his art. They would have us thrust him from the stage, back into the "chokey"—the solitary cell of artistic muzzling. This is to be expected, for artists and prophets can never hope to be popular. The world is suspicious of mirrors. Perhaps the twisted mirrors of sideshow and circus can be countenanced, for they can be laughed at when they show the lean as fat and the obese as emaciated. It's the true glass that rankles us—the one that magnifies every crack and crevice, in which all the sags and bags of mortality can be clearly seen. In the presence of such a mirror, man takes out his hammer and swings it wildly. It is a little strange that we Christians whose way in the early days of Christianity was one of renunciation of the world—asserting that it is vile and depraved —should feel called upon to defend today's world from its defamers.

Those Christians who indignantly defend contemporary society against the Behans of the world give evidence that they feel with Voltaire's idiotic Doctor Pangloss that this is the best of all possible worlds. This is not quite defensible in the light of historical evidence and in the purview of Christian thought.

Looking for the kingdom of God in the smoky mirrors of hell is neither terribly original nor awfully shocking. Dante did an admirable job of this and it has represented a major area of search for God-seekers since. The Flemish playwright, Michel de Ghelderode, talking of finding God through blasphemy, is not so shocking, for despite the sharp cries, the shrill wails of the prudish and the easily shocked, Christ is always to be found consorting with the sinners and outcasts of the world. The damning indictments of respectability as found in the works of Bloy and Bernanos should warn the sincerely searching artist away from the shoals of respectability where the waters are placid but shallow, and the revolutionary ideals of Christianity lack maneuvering room. Many a great potential artist has foundered on these shoals.

Of course, it's not only Brendan Behan who bellows with the misanthropic shout, "To hell with you all, you rotten undeserving creatures of a stinking world." The Irish, naturally, are wonderfully good at it. Their invective is colorful and their wit is bold and wild. Since Shaw started boxing the ears of what he considered a society of mental slovens, the Irish, home and abroad, have managed to be in the thick of it. Shaw really turned out to be the greatest master of theatrical misanthropy since Molière despite the fact that there is in all of Shaw a big-hearted puckishness under the tough surface that makes one wonder whether he's more misanthrope or tease. As a matter of fact, there are times when, for instance, as you watch *Saint Joan* or *Captain Brassbound's Conversion,* when you are forced to wonder, "Isn't this really a romantic old fraud playing anarchist?"

However, there's misanthropy and there's misanthropy. Behan, shaking his fist at heaven, at the law, and at the St. Vincent de Paul Society, is not to be mistaken for Shaw, and there's a bitterness that toughens the grain a little—that changes the gaiety. Under the madcap humor there's not so much Shaw's stinging barb but a whetted blade. Behan doesn't want to grab your intellect, he wants to change the world.

Taking the analogy along a bit further, if it's true that Behan carries a sharp sword, Shelagh Delaney, writer of *A Taste of Honey*, hides a poisoned dart and carries it pointed at the heart of the world. She's not so much out to change society as to poison it.

Again like Behan, here's a writer who understands some of the principles of humor and who manages to get the audience to laughing, but there's a ghoulishness in her humor that makes as much for nausea as for gaiety. Here, in *A Taste of Honey*, is a view of life so personal and so jaundiced that we cannot really find human compassion, the much needed ingredient if a play is really to strike fire in the audience member's heart. Like Thornton Wilder, we don't really care about the "adulteries of dentists" or the fornications of Lancashire working girls either, for that matter. Something must broaden the problems of the characters over into our area of struggle—of concern—or we just can't bring ourselves to care and the whole thing becomes much like watching a dog being run over by a car . . . a car that backs over him again and again until there are bloody guts all over the avenue. It's neither eloquent nor entertaining.

Purely personal misanthropy is vastly inferior to social denunciation. Behan's wild invective is vastly more useful as an introduction to compassion or enticer to action than Shelagh Delaney's morbid self-pity. Behan and Shaw always manage to put their characters into a frame—into human context so that we may recognize them and see how they relate to us. Delaney's Helen and Josie sound too much like a *melange* of self-pity and self-justification to move us. It's nearly impossible to feel like helping or even sympathizing with one who talks about nothing but himself and who whines and moans at every step. The only appeal the play really has, as a result of this, is a spurious one. Some of us are tantalized by the brash vulgarity of the work and by the fact that a nineteen-year-old girl who lives with her mother could have written it. We claim that it entertains us lest we be thought prudish, but when all is said and done, it leaves us cold.

In the misanthropy of England's "Angry Young Men" we also find attempted self-justification and the destructive kind of disgust that makes one more ill than rightfully wrathful. There have always been angry young men and there have been times in the history of our civilization when their anger resulted in much good or the cure of much that was wrong. Aristophanes, Chaucer, Rabelais, Molière, Dean Swift, Synge and Gogol were all at times very angry young men, all subject to a certain misanthropy. Their vitriol, however, was purposefully directed toward the improvement of the world—the reform of manners and morals—and not toward a carping self-justification chopping down everything else so that they could stand straight and tall like a midget in a morgue. Their misanthropy wasn't self-pitying like that of Osborne and the others. It didn't hack away at man for being silly bourgeois but for being hypocritical and full of cant and falsehood. The bourgeois isn't contemptible because he's dull and tiresome, but because he's small and mean of soul. It's no moral crime to be boring but it is to have a cramped, pinched soul with no room for love.

John Osborne is a technically interesting young playsmith for example. He delineates the middle class in savagely denunciatory terms. He rips at them and demolishes their wants and their ways. But at root, Osborne is self-pitying sensationalist in his work. He gets a great deal of attention, just like any man who shouts "Fire!" in a crowded bus, but he really doesn't manifest any knowledge of what he doesn't like, where he wants to go, or what humanity really is. He's like the man who only knows what he reads in the papers— no insight—no human vision. For a playwright this is a regrettable form of impotency.

Being angry is perfectly all right. There's a lot to be angry with, but when it's done for effect, to build the ego, or with no real norm of what life *ought* to be, it's like taking one's pants off in public. It draws a lot of attention, but it doesn't make much sense.

So perhaps we can stay with Behan in looking for a proper denouncer. To be sure he's petulant and visceral. To be sure he enjoys sloshing around in the fetid swamp, but at least he's got some vision of what ought to be. He knows the norms for what's human and what's right. Without such a norm, writing a play is like turning a trained monkey loose on a typewriter. Something worthwhile may result, but the odds are a little on the long side.

Though Behan may never prove a major gunboat in the fleet of satire, he will never founder on the shoals of respectability, for he sails deep waters. Though he lacks draught, and though he may someday swamp on one of his defiant voyages, he navigates well and as he sails, blasphemously thumbing his nose at the heavens, over the bay of art, he proves that his arrogant nose has caught the scent of God's great sea beyond.

Chapter Eight

For Love of a Lecture

Drama Goes "Epic"

THE professional theatre, as we know it, is a gloomy, dingy place. The gilt flakes from its unattended baroque walls, the curtains hang rich but rotten. Yet we who follow that old bawd, theatre, keep dragging ourselves back to it in the hope that divine lightning may now and then strike. It is a rare thing, but a wonderful thing when it happens, and the dreary business of seeing the same faces, sitting cramped in the same balding plush seats, and of experiencing the same threadbare banalities opening after opening, can evaporate under exposure to genuine talent, to real art, to sincere inspiration.

Ours has recently been a theatre of sensation and emotion. There have been good productions and there have been bad productions, but in general we have seen an appalling lack of quality in past years. It has been a strange two-headed theatre with floods of irrelevancy—plays with little or nothing to do with the problems of contemporary man—*or* with the droll Quixotic vision of thoughtful, serious playwrights riding Realism's dead nag, trying vainly to take the hurdles of profundity and intelligence on a charger that can't charge, much less take the jump. Since Shaw, real intelligence and the technique to bear it has gone out of our theatre to be replaced by a monopoly of sense and emotion.

Into the void has moved the so-called theatre of the *avant garde*, nihilistic faddists, clever descendants of Pirandello and the addled Antonin Artaud, who seek to shock—to challenge —to blow down our theatrical house of straw without a new structure to take its place. They bring, as Edward Albee, one of their bellwethers recently bleated. ". . . no solutions, only complaints."

For those of us who shudder at the thought of what these men bring, there is yet cause for hope. This past season or two has marked the influx of a new drama—right on Broadway, the much-maligned Main Street of our theatrical aspiration—that promises to draw us back to a theatre where mind, heart, and sensation may again conspire to draw an audience "up and outside itself" in the theatre—a conspiracy of completeness that enhances life and makes it richer for having been so illuminated onstage.

Many of us are not fully aware of it and many of us are a trifle disturbed at the strange things happening in our theatre, but yet something revolutionary is certainly taking place under our noses. Our flagging theatre is slowly but surely being revitalized by a force called, somewhat spuriously, "epic theatre"—a flawed form many of us had thought but the errant affectation of a weathervane Marxist named Bertolt Brecht.

Who would have dreamed that from the fusty beer halls of Munich and Berlin of the twenties there would come a clean, clear breath of inspiration to regenerate the sagging stage of the sixties and the dreary decade that came before? Who would have imagined that the seeds of a new ascendant theatre would shoot up from the tangled roots of Vorticism, of dadaism, of Leger's theories of art, of Corbusier's "functionalism," and the artistic atrocities of George Grosz who was once jailed for drawing Christ with a gas mask? And finally, who would have looked for a cigar-smoking, denim-clad Marxist bustling around the foundations beneath our new theatre of intellect, integrity, and inspiration?

Yet it is so, and the author of the most talked about and marvelled at of the new dramas, Robert Bolt whose *A Man For All Seasons* became an electric sensation on "the Great White Way," speaks of Bertolt Brecht as a major influence in his work. In the spare musculature of this superb play and several other works by a handful of playwrights in the last two seasons, "epic" influences seem very much in evidence. *Gideon, Irma La Douce, The Wall, Becket, Advise and Consent, The Visit,* and *First Love* have all shown evidences of having "epic" ink in their dramaturgical veins. Nearly a dozen dramatists have started swinging confidently down the lane taken several years back by many contemporary stage designers. The designers really started what is now becoming a movement. Designers have often done just this in the history of the theatre.

The so-called "epic theatre" found its name and initial style when the leftist playwright, Alfons Paquet, and a Marxist director, Erwin Piscator, joined forces in 1926 to produce Paquet's play *Sturmflut*. This play, dealing with revolution and the dynamics of Marxist dialectic, employed a number of new techniques—techniques unfamiliar and downright shocking to orthodox practitioners of theatre art. Piscator and Paquet conjured up film effects, narrative gimmicks, and a primitive sort of emotional alienation that created a drama with remarkable fluidity, cinematographic swiftness, and an amazing clarity of thought.

Popularizing this evolving and very experimental technique was left to Bertolt Brecht, a brash young poet from Munich, whose years of work with the famous *Berliner Ensemble* have attracted world attention and whose much talked of "alienation theory" or "A-effect" has excited the curiosity and sometimes indignation of the theatre world. Brecht, with an amazing record of production and authorship prior to his death in 1956, put the term "epic" in the theatre vocabulary and fascinated the critics and theorists of Europe and even, to a lesser extent, those of America, with the audacity of his thought.

Basically, Brecht's idea was that the contemporary theatre audience had become too passive. He felt that they sit like sponges, soaking up vicarious experience in the theatre, suspending thought and judgment, becoming, in short, inhuman. In order to restore their dignity—in order to keep them intellectually alive and acute, Brecht felt it necessary to keep them *aware* of the social act of the play—of the artifice of theatre. He felt that they should constantly be reminded that they are in a theatre. He felt that whenever they became too emotionally involved for proper judgment that the dramatist should kick them awake with some overtly theatrical device to put the derailed intellect back on the track. He sought a theatre in which the audience would go out, intellectually enriched and morally involved. In short, for Brecht, catharsis, the traditional physic of emotion, would not suffice.

Furthermore, Brecht felt that our theatre had become fat and flabby. He felt that the accretions of realism had forced our playwrights to irrelevancy. Thus we sit through ten utes of banal conversation about window drapes or filter tips in order to discover one eloquent line. We are forced to listen to an eight-minute telephone conversation by some inane housemaid in order to get a few seconds worth of exposition. Brecht felt that the theatre, in order to revitalize itself, must strip away much of this needless flab and return to the basic facts of theme and plot—the spine of the play.

Much has been made of the bizarre aspects of Brecht's theory. His "epic" concept of simultaneity in which simultaneous action explores the various possibilities of a scene, his extensive use of projection, his idea that the actor must be clearly *imitating* and never "within the skin of the part." There are other, even more far-fetched things to be found in his works—critical and theoretical works, that is—but it is our good fortune that Brecht was vastly more talented as a playwright than as a theorist.

His best known plays in America, *The Good Woman of Setzuan*, *The Threepenny Opera*, *Mother Courage*, *Galileo*, and *The Caucasian Chalk Circle* are lean and dramatically valid plays which fulfill the overall aims of Brecht's theorizing, but avoid the pitfalls of his more bizarre ideals. Technically, he has shown a new path to those who would fashion a drama more in keeping with man's rationality than that which floods our theatre today—a drama in which the mind is not lulled to sleep, but one in which it is encouraged to stay watchfully aware. Parenthetically, it is fortunate that we *do* stay alert in the theatre of Brecht, for the star to which he has shackled his muse is incandescently "red."

The "epic" ideal is not as radical as it may sound, for our own American playwright and scholar, Thornton Wilder, did something of the same sort in his immortal *Our Town*. Whenever it appears that we are to become swept up in the emotional bathos of George and Emily's love, the stage manager interrupts us with a reminder that we are knee deep in reminiscence—we are in the make-believe world of the theatre.

As Robert Bolt says in the preface to the published version of *A Man For All Seasons*, "The style I eventually used was a bastardized version of the one most recently associated with Bertolt Brecht." He goes on to say that, ". . . the style practiced by Brecht differs from the style taught by Brecht, or taught to us by his disciples."

In *A Man For All Seasons* it seems that Bolt has chosen the better part of what Brecht has offered us. Avoiding both the stark "alienation" of Brechtian theory in which one deliberately seeks to alienate the audience from any sympathy with character or situation, *and* the deliberate "shock" effect of the *avant garde* theatre, Bolt startles us with humaneness. He amazingly enough surprises us with a vision of our own wonderful humanity—the thought and spirit we have long been led to wonder about. Where indeed had it gone? Our theatre has not illuminated man's intellect and spirit lately. Bolt, with the "spare verbal architecture" of his story, with the clean and beautiful theatrical convention that sits on his shoulder like a ministering angel, brings us a fresh revelation of the potential of man. The humanity we thought we had lost is returned to us.

A Man For All Seasons tells the story of Sir Thomas More, of whom Samuel Johnson said, "He was the person of the greatest virtue these islands ever produced." It tells us also the story of the superbly civilized man of sense and sensibility, More, on whom the Church conferred an even more authoritative canonization and called "saint."

Too often a saint's life in the theatre is rendered with a heavy-handed piety comprehensible only in terms of the tackiest emotional empathy. Instead of ink, the saint's tale is most often penned in honey. The beautiful "folly of the cross" concept to which we are all challenged is depicted with a sort of euphoric glow of golden sentiment that suggests sanctity to be a high form of birdwatching sanctioned by some celestial Audubon Society. In fact, in the hands of most play and film makers, it is rendered sugary, over-emotional, and singularly unmanly. It's to be admitted that many saints have been biographically interpreted for us as downright distasteful—sugar and cream sissies or thundering demagogues. Though some may have been these things, neither being completely inconsistent with sanctity, neither extreme is intrinsic to sainthood. Humanity, however, the completeness of soul-body union, is.

99

In Bolt's inspired evocation of More, sanctity looks a great deal like good "horse sense"—or better, good "man sense." Thomas More, Lord Chancellor of England under the amorous autocrat, Henry VIII, cannot find it in his conscience to subscribe to the Oath of Supremacy that King Harry prescribes for More and every other "loyal" subject. Putting the inviolability of his conscience before physical safety, Thomas goes before heaven's tribunal for a martyr's crown after exhausting the protection of man's tribunal where perjury had chased him from the refuge of man-made law. Thomas goes through the bloody block to God while his contemporaries—so many of them—sell their heavenly birthright, like Esau, for the thin porridge of self-preservation.

And as Bolt's Thomas goes to the almost inevitable fork in the road where God's interests and Caesar's diverge, we see in him so much humanity, so much homeliness and wit, so much kindly good humor, that the business of sanctity and the business of the heroic moral choice comes very close to us and the play says, despite the great chasm of time, something most applicable in this hour of history when individual consciences have been melted for butter and are traded over the counters of commerce.

Even beyond the superb content of *A Man For All Seasons*, however, there are other things that make this a magnificent production of a great new play. Aside from its significance, the timeliness of its theme, the understated virtuosity of Paul Scofield's acting, and all its other marvellous credits, it has the virtue of arresting theatricality. It is one of those shows that tell you from the opening curtain that you are to be immensely pleased—royally entertained. In the frame of narration—another basically "epic" device—in Bolt's stage-manager-like character, the Common Man, we are cajoled and kidded and teased and unerringly led through the thickets of law, secular and divine, that characterize the story of the good Sir Thomas.

In the hands of Robert Bolt, the "epic" touch remains hard and dry but not cynical. Brecht depicts, in his theatre, the man of wandering hands—neighbor's pocket, the blouse of his best friend's wife, his parent's throat—and wavering loyalties. Bolt depicts the steadfast man, the man who moves and bends with the complexities of living and yet reserves some small part—some modest rock of rectitude for himself and his nature as a creature of God. This contrast demonstrates, it seems, that Bolt is a sort of theatrical Aquinas, Christianizing the new mimetic Aristotle, Brecht. If the analogy is too painful for either Scholastics or Marxists, we may at least admit that Bolt has wrought something new and wonderful from the raw materials of artifice given by Brecht.

All sorts of first principles have been stated for the theatre. All sorts of interpretations have been given to them once they have been expounded in the first place so that theatrical disputation most often takes place in the midst of a semantic jungle that is as impenetrable as it is frightening to those who are content simply to attend theatre with the hope of enjoying plays. There nevertheless seems a certain consensus amid all the babble, that in the theatre we seek to illuminate man, that poor stumbling cruciform creature we all represent. If this is indeed true and our theatre, beneath her bangles and glitter, serves to show us ourselves as God made us, then it could well be that the tool of "epic theatre" has been well-placed in the strong, able hands of playwright Robert Bolt.

Chapter Nine

Sweet Bird Named Success

The Vision of Tennessee Williams

Tennessee Williams is still a man who asks too little of love. In one of his recent creations for the theatre, *Period of Adjustment*, a play which had been hailed by many as presaging a "new" Williams, we find a work still unfulfilled as a search for the level of life that America's most controversial playwright seems so driven to seek.

Though the feverishness has changed its range from aberration and perversion to a relatively healthy heterosexualism and all the characters of the piece are married, Williams has changed only in what appears to be a grinning satisfaction that his characters have found a resolution of relative happiness. Again we see a playwright who is content to work out all the world's problems on one of the brilliantly executed beds that stage designer Jo Mielziner seems so readily to supply. This play, like most of his other works, gives no indication that its creator has seen or would recognize any sort of love above the purely physical. He persists in manifesting a childlike entrancement with the ideology of Freud though the world has long since matured enough to realize that though Freud had and still has value, he is not necessarily gospel. Adler's concept of man's *urge for power* as a human motivator is still a greater influence in the theatre than his fellow psychologist's theories of sexual motivation.

In this play dealing with the adjustment of a newly married couple to each other as sex partners and an older couple's readjustment to one another in a vaguely analogous way, Williams has calmed down considerably and betrays far less hysteria in his search for the meaning of life. He relaxes enough to toss a few satiric brickbats at society here and there and he has kept his form of expression well within the bounds of comedy. Despite the basic sincerity that has always kept Williams above the level of the mere sensationalists and despite the fact that there are some piddling evidences of continuing search, the writer of this latest play shows a considerable satisfaction with man, on the fleshy level of existence that, like riddled wings, prevents him from soaring to the levels he has come close to in earlier works. Even with a potential for soaring, Williams seems happy in *Period of Adjustment*, to keep his wings folded and to slosh about with small, personal things.

Normally, Williams is a sack of questions—good questions, searching and excitingly stated questions, eschatological questions digging deep beneath the rubble that contemporary thought has become. To say, however, that Tennessee Williams has a point of view is to mistake a relative period of calm for a complete rest, a temporary cessation of wishing for an absolute satisfaction of all desires.

Period of Adjustment is much on the order of an unsatisfactory draw. An approximate sort of equilibrium has been found, but no one—Williams, his fans or his critics—seems very happy about it. In the gospel of the prophet Sigmund he has sought the meaning of life, though even in this he has not pressed the search very hard. With the half-heartedness of this "new Williams" he has denied himself entrance into the real world of Freud and is perfectly happy sitting outside contemplating ladies' undergarments.

Despite the superficiality of his Freudianism in this play, one can see that Williams feels, at least for now, that the meaning of human life is to be found in the area. The love and sensitivity which he asks of life and the "something wild" he nostalgically looks for in *Orpheus Descending* and other works—some of the one-act plays and in the preface to *Twenty-Seven Wagons*—are apparently to be found between the covers of a bed rather than in those of the books of Christian revelation. In this regard, *Period of Adjustment*, the spoor of the "new Williams" seems to be the sign of a great lull in the search that Williams has been violently conducting in the years of his prominence. Perhaps *Period of Adjustment* represents a sort of final solution—a terminus of all search, for in the final curtain's apparent sexual adjustment there is at least a relative order.

If one is to accept the writer of *Period* as the truly "new" man, this would, to this critic's mind, be a most unfortunate thing, for until Williams finds man and the true meaning of life, any slackening of pace—any period of calm—will further hold back what many of us hope to be a momentous public evolution toward truth in the mind of this powerful theatre artist. If Williams is willing to stop with this type of play and its pat commercial answer (though it has closed on Broadway, it has become a favorite summer stock piece) then we have lost an artistic giant, one who constantly chafes our consciences, and have gained a pretentious George Axelrod. If the relative cosiness of the connubial bed is to be equated with the answer Williams has sought through his early plays then we may look back with great longing to the sincerity of his incest-cannibalism-homosexuality stage of development.

There is, however, some reason for optimism. One can hope, from a few signs scattered around in this sometimes amusing and sometimes erotic comedy, that the search will continue and though Williams has here mistaken the narrow range of sex for the terrible breadth of love, there are certain other elements of magnitude remaining.

For example, one of the characters states that man is born under a question mark, a question mark posing three great questions: "Where did we come from? Why? Where are we going?" Though the thought is hardly original, the fact that he has chosen to put it in this comedy of the *boudoir* indicates a further goal yet unattained—a question yet unanswered beyond the superficial "adjustment" of the moment. In a second act curtain line, when a nervous new bride clasps a statue of the Infant of Prague to her breast and speaks of her loneliness to Him, we see in Williams at least a hint of the further possibilities of love, though at the same time it is the sloppily sentimentalizing Williams whom we met earlier in *The Rose Tattoo* and in the chaotic *Camino Real*. In *Period* he talks too of the modern suburbanite living like a vegetable sitting poised over a great underground cavern into which his home is gradually sinking, content with his TV Westerns and his doped beer. In this, too, when the poetry pulls out slightly ahead of the banality, we see something of Williams' disgust with the world—his serious and somewhat confused moral purpose.

Some have claimed that the even more recent *The Night of*

the Iguana represents a truly matured Williams, a wise and balanced Williams, a play of real profundity and style. Perhaps in a way it does represent a Williams wandering back *toward* the general directions of his earlier search and a sort of antidote to the cheapness, the smug infantilism of *Period of Adjustment,* but to infer that it offers wisdom or even hope is to exaggerate grossly.

The Night of the Iguana with its blatant symbolism and its again allegorical characters is another tour of grotesquerie, but this time the characters seem false, the gore is painted gore, the wounds are prosthetic wounds, and the bruises are tipped on with a brush. The small-calibre solution still dogs our man and again he hints at small consolations in place of overflowing love. It's as though Williams, the bloody and yet unbowed Williams, has returned to the scenes of past triumph —to the hungry nightmare landscape that made him—but this time he wears a Chesterfield coat, a Homburg hat, and he knows (and he hopes we won't recognize it) that he's a victim of his own success. This time he's replaced Val Xavier's yearning for innocence, Tom Wingfield's dream of self-expression, and Chance Wayne's gamble for a glorious future, for a man's attempt to revenge himself on a mother who punished him for self-abuse and a God who wrapped his throat in a Roman collar.

In this play, the "new Williams" is pressing to recapture the old Williams, but the high priests of the theatre will not take back the tainted silver.

In Williams' past monstrous dissatisfaction with the world we have seen his power and his principal virtue. As in our own Christian cultural history, we did not develop significantly into the areas of art and literature until we realized the world was unrepentant even in the light of the redemption—that the temporal universe would not immediately stand with Christ, and that the "Second Coming" would be delayed. When we started to gaze at the horror of sin and took our place in the unregenerated world while waiting for the uncertain time of the "Parousia," it was only then that we sowed the seeds for a cultural bloom. If Williams is satisfied with the modest good that *Period of Adjustment* affords, then we must wave him *adieu* as a dramatist of consequence and relegate him to the boulevard theatre.

In contrast to the "new Williams"—the simmered-down blast furnace—we have only to look back to 1959 to see a fiery artist, tearing away at the sensibilities of a complacent world to find the location of a conscience grown fat. The great carrion bird that Williams turned loose in theatre—*Sweet Bird of Youth*—is a moody creature that soars high, breathing smoke and flame, only to land a moment later, babbling breathlessly about inner impulses like some egotistical comedian on his analyst's couch. Monstrous, powerful, confused, violent, and laced from wingtip to wingtip with sooty streaks of the most intense color, this wild creature is perhaps the most breathtaking of the works that have spewed forth from Williams' smouldering typewriter.

Like some half-mad contemporary effort at the mixed style of the medieval drama with its allegorical characters blending sublimity with the most earthy elements, this apocalyptic vision of the dramatist Williams abounds with symbols—some compelling, some wildly effective, some vastly uncommunicative. A great rose-colored bed, smouldering pink neon lamp globes, luminescent palm leaf patterns against a blue night sky, the gigantic television image of a screaming demagogue claiming that God sent him from his native "red clay hills" to defend the virtue of white Southern womanhood; these symbols batter away at the audience with a sickeningly accurate cannonade that leaves one limp with a revelation of overwhelming evil.

Deistic in concept, the work poses the question as to when the heavens will divulge answers to eternal questions. As mentioned in an earlier chapter, in making a comparison with one of Ingmar Bergman's more deistic works, a character in this play, *Sweet Bird*, denies the intervention of God in the affairs of men, and in the early tryout version of the play, we heard the shattered movie star suggest that ". . . someday the mystery God will step down from behind his clock face like an actor divesting himself of makeup and costume." This statement and many of the statements in this strange work despairingly cry out, "God is silent, time is passing, and we are being pushed down the road to dusty death!"

In *Sweet Bird of Youth*, somewhat reminiscent of Val Xavier in *Orpheus Descending*, we have a young man in whom the seeds of destruction are sown, a young man who, in this case, had sought since he was seventeen to get by on nothing but his physical beauty and an ability to gratify women who in loneliness and need cling to him. Seeking always to "get it made" and to rise in the world with his modest gifts and his driving dreams (the typical Horatio Alger type problem for the American boy) he finds time running out on his life with the dream unfulfilled and with his body, mind, and soul rotting.

Called by the haunting vision of a first love who lives on in spiritual torment after having been unwillingly subjected to abortion and hysterectomy, he returns to his native town with the Princess Pazmezoglu, a broken-down film actress with whom he shares a trinity of anesthetic illusions: alcohol, sex, and narcotics. Dragging himself away from the degrading relationship of servant-paramour of the woman, he spends one evening vainly seeking to recapture his "sweet bird of youth" and his own sweetheart.

Unknown to him, Boss Finley, Huey Long type political boss and father of the old girl-friend, plans to have him emasculated if he doesn't leave by midnight. As the crowded hours progress he begins to realize that time and the tawdry efforts he has made to seek his "place in the sun" have already denuded him of his potency as a real man, his dreams, his potential for seeking a gleaming destiny ranging above and beyond the degradation and sordidness of his Gulf-side hometown. As the threat of real physical castration is made manifest, the symbolic castration of Chance Wayne becomes evident and he concludes the play by staying to face his torturers as he asks the audience to recognize something of him in all men.

As in *Orpheus Descending*, an earlier dark vision, Williams exposes to our gaze the naked soul of the man dying of spiritual thirst, hotly pursuing that mystery that will quench his torment, in a world that destroys the sensitive and the lost. Blanche Dubois' rape by a brutal world in the person of Stanley Kowalski, Val Xavier's wretchedly horrible fate as the blowtorch turns him into his own funeral pyre, the smouldering hopelessness of Alma Winemuller—all of these people are destroyed as illusion, honest search, and wonder are turned to ash by the merciless flames of brutality and insensitivity in this terrible world of man. In these plays, those who would dare to search for meaning and those who would dare to build illusions to cover the lack of meaning in their lives are cut down by the sated, the sadistic, and the satisfied.

The characters of Williams' world are tortured by some of the cruellest devices imaginable as they are castrated, driven mad, turned whore, burnt alive, cannibalized, raped, or sent into a dark cave of withdrawal and fear, with hope lying shattered around their feet. There are some who cannot see amongst all the screaming degradation anything but a *Grand Guignol* show with its maiming, its disfigurements, its Thyestian gore. Certainly there is something of the horror show in his plays, for watching such works as *Sweet Bird of Youth*, *Suddenly Last Summer*, and *Orpheus Descending* is like choosing a ringside seat in an accident ward. You sit there staring at the mangled, vulgarly torn shreds of tortured humanity, wishing you couldn't see it at all, but too filled with perverse fascination to look away. Sitting in the theatre you are asked to take a long level look into the eyes of the Devil.

Granting the danger to soul and mind, is there some value to such explorations of the turbid depths of human life— this cesspool view of a crawling, festering world?

Perhaps here, without straining too hard to find it, we can talk of an undisciplined, almost unconscious quest—a longing —for something half known, veiled in flesh, some breath of clear sky beyond animality and cruelty and vice. The York Crucifixion play retained its place in the line of march on Corpus Christi those many centuries ago despite its nearly blasphemous dwelling on the horrors of Christ's cruel death. It stayed in because it could be clearly seen that amidst the vile joking at the expense of the condemned God-man there was still an assessment of man, a creature free and knowing and able to choose freely between evil and good. So too, the protagonists Chance Wayne and Val Xavier, stumbling through a chamber of horrors, at least seek the clear sight of hope in some unshifting value beyond that which is known by sense alone.

In the churches of the Age of Faith were found remnants of the profane, the obscene, the vile—all strangely enough presented as reflecting meaning and order in the universe they mirrored as art. There is something in this groping search for God, for freedom from the world's taint, in *Orpheus Descending* as Val and Lady talk of a strange little sky-colored bird that never lands on earth but stays clean and untouched high in the sky near the great life-giving sun. Val says of this bird, "I'd like to be one of those birds and never be—corrupted!"

In *Sweet Bird*, the Princess Pazmezoglu talks with Chance Wayne as the clock ticks loudly and time flees past them. They talk of life and the unfulfilled longings of mankind. This, too, shows Williams to us in perhaps a new light.

Williams' own brother, a convert to Catholicism, wrote some time ago in *Information* magazine that he feels Tennessee to be a writer of morality plays. In this article called "Is Tennessee Williams Really a Catholic Playwright?" brother Walter suggests that brother Tom (his real name is Thomas Lanier Williams) does not write "dirty plays" but rather purgative plays in the traditions of the medieval and post medieval moralities which seek to improve manners and morals. Walter Williams' contention is that his brother's work shows forth the horror of evildoing and the ultimate ruin to which it leads.

Speaking up against *Williams,* critic John Chapman of the New York *News* says:

Tennessee Williams is a greatly gifted, extraordinarily original and dirty-minded dramatist who has been losing hope for the human race . . . or that part of it which does its sinning in the sunny South.

In a similar vein, but in much amplified form, critic Marya Mannes devoted a whole article in the *New York Times Sunday Magazine* to an attack on Williams and those who write like him. In this article called "More Fair Ladys?" Miss Mannes asserts that it is wrong for us to poke around the sewers and attics for our plays. She felt that one should look at the good things of the world and try, through an optimistic and humanistically assertive theatre, to cure the "fabulous invalid" of some of his contemporary woes.

These conflicting positions seem to represent Williams as something of an extreme—a moralist or a pornographer. Though he's really neither, it's not far-fetched to suggest that there's an element of both present in his work. His constant use of sexual extremes suggests that there is some intention to use sexuality deliberately as a sensational means to interest people in his works. While we cannot, in any just sense, make a hard and fast judgment in this regard, there's a great deal of evidence that points in that direction. For example, the language in *Cat on a Hot Tin Roof* goes a good deal farther than the requirements of the work seem to demand. The final line of *Period of Adjustment,* the discussions in *Rose Tattoo,* the extreme forms of sexuality in many of the plays suggest that Williams takes an extraordinary interest in sex themes and makes sex an even more important and all-pervasive thing than it is in reality. In a sense he kicks Jung and Adler out and sleeps happily with Freud.

On the other hand, Williams *does* moralize. The motion picture screenplay *Suddenly Last Summer,* based on the earlier short stageplay (Garden District) packs a moral wallop in its powerful suggestion that he who *uses* other people—who consumes them in an ego-centric excess—will in turn be fed upon. In his handling of self-delusion, a disease which seems to afflict many of his characters, there is more than a tiny hint of a warning.

To be sure, Williams is yet viewing life through a dark mirror—a fouled lens obscuring any light except the flickering flames of passion. Like the undisciplined novels of Thomas Wolfe, who also burst from the warm Southern night as an earlier Godseeker, the genius of Williams may claw a furrow in the bland face of today's theatre. For all his faults one can find the major part of his work significant—sometimes dull, sometimes beautiful, sometimes nauseating and blasphemous, salted with the vulgar, larded through with the fat of inaction and *stasis*, sometimes profound—always, however, questioning and searching for a meaning beyond a meaning. Like Alice, though he is lost amidst the wild grotesqueries of a shadowy wonderland, perhaps he can, with God's grace, drink from some magic bottle which, in bringing him to size, will grant him a true perspective on the universe.

Only in this work, *Period of Adjustment*, do we see a *caesura*—a break in the fascinating progress Williams seemed to be making. In this work, one can hope, for him, that he soon sees through the incomplete solution he proposes. As a creative artist he is required to have some understanding of man. Even in comedy, laughter is not enough in itself. Laughter without some understanding of what one laughs at and the norm from which it deviates is tantamount to idiocy. If Williams is content to maintain his understanding of man at the level of mere "flesh," then he would do well to return to the ambiguous and fragile *Glass Menagerie* or to give up playwriting and live off his royalties.

There are those who will say *Period of Adjustment* is only a comedy and doesn't mean much one way or another. It's only a brief respite for Williams—a superficial failure that can be written off.

The fallacy here lies in writing genuine comedy off as of no significance. Out of our contemporary failing to distinguish comedy from its younger sister, farce, we are deluded into thinking that comedy doesn't deal with serious matter. Real comedy is *always* serious in its object, if not in technique and theme. Williams is so sincere a playwright (or at least he has been so) that even in his most commercial efforts—in his lightest moments—he has always searched, probed, and thrust away at the soft underbelly of our neurotic society. *Period of Adjustment* may only be written off as an indicator if we take it completely out of context and forget all the other works of its creator. Though it surely does lack the vitality, the brimstone bite, it keeps the famous Williams style—the wild leaping back and forth from poetry to banality—and uses it to little purpose. It is a play that appears to have been written for commercial value alone.

The language of *Period* is erotic. Conversation that belongs in a G.I. latrine and actions that belong in the privacy of a marital bedchamber are used mainly for trimming. The talented little man from St. Louis should realize that he need not resort to such tricks in order to gain a hearing. Unless the fine talent of Williams has become reduced to a compulsion to scribble on rest-room walls, many of the lines in the play militate against the play itself.

Whatever is said of this play and those which follow it and whatever direction the so-called "new" Tennessee takes, Williams remains a glowing ember of controversy in the grab-bag of the American theatre. He is a poser of questions, a seeker of answers, and a wanderer over the hard surface of truth who cannot yet break through the crust of the apparent to the real. As one who manifests that he is being pursued by "The Hound of Heaven" perhaps this is all but a "period of adjustment" and if he doesn't become spiritually fat and artistically complacent, we may someday see a true "new" Williams spring into being. Before this happens, however, there is a need for a sharpening of perception and a hailstorm of grace.

Period of Adjustment for all its high hopes, answers no questions, asks but a few, and doesn't really change our tiger. He still burns brightly in the dark loneliness of spiritual night.

Chapter Ten

Sex in the Theatre

CHARACTERISTIC of our Catholic approach to the question of drama criticism and film criticism is an overwhelming preoccupation with the Sixth Commandment. There is no question that the theatre and film do frequently overemphasize the sexual aspect of human personality and there is considerable reason to believe that they, like many other strong stimuli, may have an aphrodisiac effect on their spectators. There is, to be quite candid about it, a certain element of moral danger to this, but one may still wonder at the hysterical attitude many Catholics have taken in this regard and wonder whether it's a fully sane, thoughtful approach to a very serious problem. That which Irish playwright Sean O'Casey has described as "the ferocious chastity of the Irish" seems to have communicated itself to all levels of American Catholic society.

Whenever practitioners of the arts engage a Catholic in conversation about the problems of "Catholic criticism" or when these same artists consider what they face in a predominantly Catholic area, the matter is always discussed in terms of the sexual content of the work.

Despite the fact that we learned of *seven* deadly sins in catechism class long ago and lust didn't head the list, one would think it the *only* sin as he overheard Catholic conversation. A good many types of evil can be depicted through the various art forms and lust is by no means an exclusive mark of any particular art media unless erotic dancing (or is it exotic?) or some other such activity can be dignified with the term "art media."

Sex has become a major preoccupation in our times. It has always been an activity of some popularity, but as a source of all-absorbing interest for careful thought, study, and conversation, its history is limited. It has become one of the major dramatic themes of our times. Almost devotedly, with a dead-seriousness, many a contemporary dramatist sets out to write deeply sexual plays as though he were a committed evangelist for something that needs to be popularized.

Sex is anything but *new* as a literary or dramatic theme, for it has consistently attracted writers throughout the ages. *Oedipus Rex, Hippolytus, Medea, Romeo and Juliet, Othello, Fuente Ovejuna, Phaedre,* and many other enduring gems of world drama have sprung forth from mainly sexual thematic material. However, in all of these plays sex was not the *only* major thematic material as it seems in so much of what is being written today. In *Oedipus* there is the major element of *hubris,* with man presuming to make himself like unto the gods—presuming to rise to meet them. This theme coexists with and essentially outweighs the incest theme which is but one facet of the basic dramatic tension. It is necessary, but provides the background rather than being an end in itself. It can in no sense be called an incest play. In *Medea* the sexual material moves into the emotion of jealousy and the motive of revenge which divorces the play from a purely sexual frame of reference. In *Romeo and Juliet* there is a strong statement for a love beyond the more sensate level.

In our day, sex has become twisted and fashioned into a major cultural force permeating the whole of our society. It stares at us from the pages of our magazines and newspapers, it blares at us from radios, it walks by us on the street in fashions clearly intended for provocation, it is the most widely employed motivational basis for almost everything in our society. It has become a national pastime and a national industry to talk about, think about, wish for, contemplate, and ask about sex. A record company currently offers housewives an album called "music to strip by" with a G-string included.

Contrary to what many people seem to think, Sigmund Freud did not invent sex, and many of the themes, actions, institutions, and works that we would today describe as Freudian long antedated his 1856 birth date. He has, however, contributed in large part to the popularization of sex as a topic of conversation, even in mixed company. Since he first posited his views and set forth his theories to the world at large, many a song-writer, many an artist, many a playwright, many an advertising man, in fact, most of us, have jumped aboard his psychiatric bandwagon with a great display of public interest in sex from a theoretical as well as experimental point of view.

Since Freud we have been regaled with sex as never before. In the words of sociologist Pitrim Sorokin:

Sexual chastity is viewed as a prudish superstition. Nuptial loyalty is stigmatized as an antiquated hypocrisy. Father is painted as a jealous tyrant desirous of castrating his sons to prevent incest with their mother. Motherhood is interpreted as "mommism" wrecking the lives of children. Sons and daughters are represented as filled with the "complexes" of seduction of their mother: and the father respectively. Sexual profligacy and prowess are proudly glamorized, *Homo sapiens* is replaced by *homo sexualis* packed with genital, anal, oral, and cutaneous libidos. The traditional "child of God" created in God's image is turned into a sexual apparatus powered by sex instinct, preoccupied with sex matters, aspiring for, and dreaming and thinking of, sex relations. (*The American Sex Revolution*).

Our advertising is based on desires for sexual experience with the constant inference that if we use the right sort of bath powder, drive the right sort of motor car, use the right fertilizer and crabgrass killer, we'll get the opportunity to sleep with all the lovely young things that seductively clutter up advertisements of everything from lingerie to tombstones. A God-given and beautiful aspect of our human nature is presented as the *whole* of our human nature—self-justifying and inviolable.

Naturally enough, our drama has in no way escaped from this creeping sexualization and it is surely as present on our stages as it is elsewhere in our culture.

Sex has always been conspicuously present in the theatre. The drama of our Western civilization actually sprang forth from the fertility worship of the ancient Egyptians and Greeks. The great God of Egypt, Osiris, and the Attic fertility deity, Dionysius, were worshipped with phallic representation and it was largely through worship of the procreative force of all nature that comedy came into being. Comedy has always had an underlying sex symbolism in its most classic forms as it becomes a potency contest with the old and impotent being outclassed by the young and fertile or with the handsome young man overcoming adversity to wed and bed the lovely young thing who is married to a crotchety and, by implication, impotent old man.

Perhaps the best example of the classic "potency *vs.* impotency" theme in comedy is Niccolō Machiavelli's *Mandragola*. This example of the "refined" theatre of the Italian Renaissance has all the classic elements of the bawdy streak that runs through our theatre. The inevitable triangle of young wife, panting young man, and elderly husband is manipulated with great skill, but it still runs true to form. The young man gets the girl and the old husband is gulled completely. This is the traditional pattern of the theatre when it speaks of sex.

There are still signs of this sort of thing in the contemporary theatre in the work of George Axelrod and playwrights of this type. To be sure, in our contemporary theatre it is either a matter of killing off the old man in a kindly way or what is threatened never quite takes place. The sweet girl's maidenly virtue or wifely continence is preserved at the last minute after the matter has been satisfactorily exploited for two and a half acts. This sort of theatrical Onanism is considered in our modern world far more respectable than letting things take their natural course.

The majority of our modern sex plays, however, are dead serious things in which two anxious, fouled-up hypochondriacs find themselves or (if you prefer to be Chekhovian) fail to find themselves through sexual adjustment. William Inge is perhaps the most skilled practitioner of this sort of thing.

Most dramatic historians agree that our Western drama did indeed grow out of the various manifestations of the Dionysiac fertility cult with its worship of the phallus and its dithyrambic songs extolling the things of earth and the body. On the very earliest artifacts available to us, tracing the history of the theatre, phallephoric figures appear, indicating more than just an incidental relationship between sex and the early mimic rituals which matured into full-blown theatre. The Greeks were very much aware of the beauties of the human body and venerated it for its reflection of the great creative beauty through which the divine spark of life is transmitted and received. In its ideal form this was not a deleterious thing, nor was it in any sense a debasement, but rather a sincere religious thankfulness for the germinal process of nature as embodied in all the corporeal orders of creation: vegetable, animal, and human.

Despite this ideal of Dionysiac worship, as with all things touched by men, there was a certain vulgarization away from the original meaning and ideals and the mimic worship at times became orgiastic with ceremonies terminating in sexual excesses, drunkenness, and assorted debaucheries. The phallus worn by the principal actor who played Omrikos, or Dionysius, became a figure of vulgar amusement and was appended to other actors.

Throughout the early period of Greek drama and well into the theatre of ancient Rome, the sexual element of theatre persisted. This was particularly so in the work of the mime comedians of the popular theatre. Without benefit of the old worship, the sex symbols remained and became something markedly different than the religious symbols they once had been. Even in the work of the writers of genuine drama, as for example Aristophanes, libidinous references were made again and again. Sex humor became a lively part of the works of Aristophanes, Menander, and the Roman comic writers, Plautus and Terence.

With the advent of Christianity with its code of general sexual abstinence and chastity, a great conflict arose. Nudity, erotic dancing, and the all-too-graphic representation of fornication aroused the indignation of the Church fathers. Even the plays that dealt with the gods delved heavily into the matter of sexual profligacy as practiced by the gods themselves. This could hardly be countenanced by the then ascendant Christians who were trying to infiltrate society with the rather unfamiliar concept of a love above the purely physical level and with a new respect for women. St. John Chrysostom and St. Cyprian lashed out at the mimes as did Martial, Macrobius, and many others.

Chrysostom said of the theatre, "Here are to be seen naught but fornication, adultery, courtesan women, men pretending to be women, and soft-limbed boys." He spoke with fervor of the theatre as a stimulator of sexual excess. He was not alone in such condemnation, as Tertullian called the theatre "the home of Venus and Liber" and Lactantius talked of the exhibitions of adultery which "so lead from fiction to fact."

Perhaps we can say that these fathers of the ancient Church

functioned as the first Catholic drama reviewers though it's to be doubted that they bothered going to see any of the shows they so vigorously denounced. At least we can hardly call them "aisle sitters."

Without doubt the Roman theatre made full commercial use of sex. Man has not changed much over the years of his history. Some of the theatre managers of ancient Rome, like some of the managers and producers of today, were willing to exploit sensationalism now and then to please their audiences and to pack the jaded citizens of the Empire into their theatres. Audiences get what they pay to see and the sexualized Roman audience voted at the box office for depravity. That's precisely what they got.

And so it went on. The *Commedia* of Renaissance Italy with its mischievous rogues and its promiscuous maidservants, the seduction comedies of the court theatres of the day (*Mandragola* represents this), the violent plays of Elizabeth's England (and who could write a more sensational sex play than Shakespeare's *Antony and Cleopatra?*)—all of them brought the audiences of antiquity their vicarious sex pleasure and the vision of their fellow man's foibles.

With Oliver Cromwell and the Puritan Commonwealth came a temporary suspension of *all* theatrical activity from 1642 till 1660. Leading up to this suppression were numerous writings by English clergymen despairing at the abuses represented in "that temple of Satan," the theatre. Many of the descriptions of the stage of the day are very like those of the early Roman fathers, though in their zealous exaggeration and in the hysteria of their invective, they go far beyond their predecessors.

In 1632, a Puritan named William Prynne published a denunciatory work called *Histrio-Mastix,* an eleven hundred page tome denouncing the stage and its immoral plays and players. Prynne had somehow found out virtually everything there was to know about the malefactions of actors, the sexual abuses perpetrated by them, the immoral intent of the plays etc. Like some of our religious critics of today, Prynne was rather contemptuous of the moral character of the players and so stated that women actors in London were all "notorious whores." At the time the book was published, Queen Henrietta Maria was rehearsing for an amateur dramatic presentation. The slur cost Prynne his ears. He was branded as a seditious libeller on both cheeks, condemned to life imprisonment, and as stated, got his ears amputated. It's likely that no libeller was ever so sternly punished.

At any rate, with the accession of Puritans like Prynne to power, the theatre was halted for a time and only now and then, through the action of opera, could anyone get even the tiniest glimpse at the art of the stage.

In 1660, with the restoration of the monarchy, the theatre returned and with it was unleashed a torrent of refined and not-so-refined sex drama which certainly "made up for lost time." It was a theatre that revelled in cuckoldry, in sly seduction, and with titillating sex talk. Its players gained a remarkable reputation for prostitution and various other moral lapses, and it was, as any canny student of human nature might guess, vastly more nasty than the theatre which was first suppressed by the "Roundheads."

And so it is obvious, with a mere skimming over part of our theatre's history, that sex drama has a long, if not venerable history.

Perhaps the first rational guide in regard to prudence in sexual matters as applied to the American theatre was provided by Father Wilfred Parsons, S.J., in *America*. In an article entitled "Bad Plays and Good Morals" in 1925, the priest cogently considered the problem of just what constitutes a proximate occasion of sin. This, of course, is the greatest problem to be encountered in this matter of sex in the theatre. Shock has nothing to do with morals. It is not a question of being shocked or even a matter of a scene or a character being distasteful to us. It is rather a question of whether or not the matter onstage will incite the normal, adult audience member to sin, either inwardly or outwardly.

Father Parson's article explains clearly and concisely the problem of this sort of exposure. Perhaps the major defect, in this article, like others of its kind, is that Father Parsons back in 1925 could give no help to the play-goer in advance to help him decide whether or not the particular play or production would constitute an occasion of sin for *him*. At this time there was virtually no source of regular play reviewing or film criticism to give the Catholic play-goer any help in this regard.

Of course, this question of advance warning is the whole *raison d'etre* of Catholic play reviewing. (Note that I said *reviewing*.) No one can really determine whether a given production will become an occasion of sin for him except in certain extreme cases. Neither can one tell whether a trip to the beach, a party, a trip downtown for shopping, or going on a business trip will constitute such an occasion of sin. It is impossible to determine this accurately, say on the basis of advertising or on the word of those associated with the production. Often the advance advertising on a play is released long before a line of actual dialogue is ever committed to paper and those hoping to attend during the first two or three months are forced to write for tickets prior to the first rehearsal.

Motion picture advertising is often so misleading, in several directions, that a perfectly wonderful show, one that may be a positively fine influence on its audiences, will appear suspect on the basis of its advertising, whereas another which may involve all sorts of morally harmful material will look relatively innocuous. Of course, in the latter case, the harm is likely not sexual, for whenever any sexual material is involved, no matter how negligible, the motion picture press agents take full advantage.

Now some will say that we should refrain from attending virtually any show merely on this basis—with this limited criteria. They will maintain that there is risk involved in any theatrical presentation and we should therefore refrain from the theatre entirely. Lest the reader think this is far-fetched, one must remember that many a suppression has been occasioned by sincere and religious people who think just that. This was the attitude of the Puritans prior to the Supression of 1642. It is rather significant to note that in 1660 when the theatre did return under license to Charles II, that it returned in a form that made the pre-Suppression stage look like a catechetical exercise.

Adopting such an attitude means that we willingly forego art in order to avoid all possible spiritual risk. This is not particularly Christian nor is it even particularly rational. We cannot be assured maximum security of any kind in this world and we must at times trust God and our own moral sense. The theatre is eminently worthwhile in the development of "the whole man" and we must remember that there is an element of risk—physical, mental, and spiritual—in the business of living itself. This fearful, suspicious attitude reminds me of a scene I saw in a supermarket some years ago.

An attractive and apparently intelligent young woman and her small son were waiting to check out a cart full of groceries. The child, around five or six and somewhat tired, put his hand on the check-out stand to lean on it. The mother told him not to touch the counter. She said, "There are germs on it. Don't touch it."

Shifting his point of support he asked, "Are there any here?"

"There are germs everywhere," the mother replied. "Everything has germs on it."

Though the woman undoubtedly had the child's best interests at heart, any bystander couldn't help wondering, if mother's hygienic immoderacy wasn't going to harm the little boy. A child growing up worrying about the germs on everything he touches is not likely to lead a very happy or fruitful existence. The analogy, carried over to the field of communications, is not hard to match among Catholics.

As Father Gardiner puts it:

I am firmly convinced that not a few Catholics, readers and critics, do considerable harm to the reputation of Catholic intelligence by forgetting that any normal, well-balanced reader can be solidly enough grounded in faith and morals and taste not to find some vulgar expressions or some frankly descriptive passages sources of "mental and moral infection."

Father Gardiner is particularly noteworthy amongst Catholic critics for his singular realization that it is not "only the Sixth Commandment shrugged out of existence by modern amoralists." There is real danger that we will become so preoccupied with irrelevant sex detail in our judgments that we will miss the deeper dangers hidden beneath the surface of the work.

For instance, in the play *Death of a Salesman* by Arthur Miller, there is some measure of sexual reference—the woman in the hotel with Willie, clad in black lace lingerie, the two whores the boys take up with in the restaurant, the discussion of Hap and Biff's bedroom exploits. There is, in addition to this, a welter of profanity recurring throughout the play. Though there may be, and I doubt it, a measure of danger in the sexual aspects of the script for certain weak adults and the profanity is something other than morally and aesthetically ideal, there is a far greater danger in this play that is often overlooked beneath the *minutia* of surface detail. Willie Loman, though paraded as a man, is not a human being at all. Though Miller presents him as a would-be tragic figure, Willie lacks one of the true elements of humanity: rationality. He is furthermore lacking in a free will. Man can reflect upon himself and govern himself. Willie is bereft of these qualities and as such is a lie. In this sense, *Death of a Salesman* becomes a dangerously dehumanizing play with its patent untruth. Danger of this type is vastly more subtle and perfidious because we do not gird ourselves to meet it. We scarcely know it's there.

We can see from our newspapers, our books, the dress of our modern female, the conversation in barber shops and beauty salons, the television and our cultural fare wherever we find it, that sexualization is on the increase in our society. It is not too surprising that the theatre and the film have reacted to this tide and have followed this march towards "the great big bed upon which all man's ills will be resolved." The theatre has traditionally reflected the temper of the times in which it has existed. No theatre *entrepreneur* attempts to create mores. He merely sells entertainment which he has fashioned in the shape of the times. The leering Restoration theatre was a reflection of the folkways of London of the time. Etheredge and Congreve and Farquahar and the others didn't make up the evil ways their plays demonstrate. They merely mirrored the times.

Repressive measures—the legal curtailing of the stage and screen—are not really going to solve the problem. Indeed, if we are going to attempt to correct this sexualization process by law, we should logically erect punitive legislation in regard to morality in dress, liquor intake, calendar art, television programming, choice of pictures for newspapers and magazines, and the style of ladies' undergarments. A society that permits children of twelve and thirteen to dance cheek to cheek under soft lights as they commence the amateur chiropractics of teen-age courtship has little right to blame the artist for its ills.

Now one particular area of danger in the whole question of sex in the theatre is encountered with the film because of its very nature. In regard to sexual stimuli, the screen with its selective use of close-up can so concentrate upon a single aspect of its subject and so remove a physical detail from context as to make it an extreme source of sexual provocation. As a matter of fact, our age's seeming preoccupation with the female bosom has been given great impetus by the motion picture with its chatter about "sweater girls" and appropriate shots a number of years ago. Needless to say, though the term "sweater girl" is obsolete, the idea of provoking with the bosom seems even stronger in today's motion pictures and the sweater has been all but removed.

Another point in regard to the sexual danger to be encountered in the movies today has to do with the nature of the illusion. Unlike theatre-going in a legitimate playhouse which is a social experience with the presence of the rest of the audience clearly acknowledged in a reasonably high degree of house illumination, the movie fan sits in almost complete darkness in a state of virtual isolation. He is called upon for no real response and is thus far more passive than the theatre-goer. He does not rise for intermissions nor is he accorded the dignity of being part of a dressed gala audience. He is instead encouraged to be a solitary dreamer lost in an impersonal darkness. It takes no profound knowledge of psychology to realize that this is an attitude most conducive to sexual response. This is a problem for those who would think in terms of what sexual material can do to our youth. It would seem in this regard that some sort of responsibility should be exercised both by movie-makers and parents to see to it that young people are not exposed to stimuli they are not prepared to cope with.

In the theatre, the situation is somewhat different. First of all, the legitimate theatre is not a children's medium of entertainment. It is neither intended for them nor is it usually priced within their range. Secondly, as previously mentioned, the theatre-goer is not alone. He is very much conscious of the persons seated with him. For this reason, he is somewhat less susceptible to the occurrences onstage—that is, those that lead to private eroticism.

Consideration of a whore onstage cannot be construed as inciting every woman in the house to become one and every man to visit one. Even when we consider her sympathetically, and we see how horrified some of our Catholic reviewers become at the thought of this, we cannot say that this makes even a moderately intelligent human being want to go out and do likewise. Art dredges out channels of consciousness and enables us to *see* more with the dispassionate eyes of the intellect, to feel more, to care more, to love more, our fellow man. Who can say that it is not a good thing for man in seeking to love his fellow? Through a vision of his sufferings, his triumphs, his fallings and failings in the theatre we are taught more of our fellow. We see him. We know him and learn better to love him. We have not been told to love the righteous woman more than the slut nor have we been told to love the moral man more than the pervert. As a matter of fact, it seems that God himself makes no differentiation amongst these and He too loves them all. Christ seemed to spend much more time on and with the lost sheep than he did on the ninety-nine left in the fold.

Now it is true that many of these themes, many of these characters, many of these actions dealing with sex, can and do constitute a danger on the stage or in the theatre. These dangers are, moreover, except in the most extreme cases, danger to children or those who are emotionally immature. Just as liquor is of great danger to the young or the unwise, so even the most discreetly handled sex theme or action *can* incite the *wrong* person to passion. It is in the exclusion of these persons that a solution to much of this social sexualization process can be found. It is safe to presume that the adult character has already been formed and it is the responsibility of the adult and his own business to keep himself untainted as best he can. It is not the business of the dramatist to be especially concerned about whether his validly artistic work may be misconstrued so as to constitute a moral danger any more than the cook need worry about whether someone will make a glutton of himself with her appetizing roast of beef.

Because in a free society we cannot legislate against "dirty thoughts," the reviewer offers his work. At least it is his function to provide the public the advance information needed so they may exclude themselves or those for whom they are responsible. He doesn't tell them whether to go or not. He merely tells them, as best he can, what the play says, what it's about, and what it looks like. It is then their judgment. It is not his function to cry down everything that may hurt a child, an incipient sex deviate, or an imaginative sinner. If he does this, then the normal may very well be denied a valuable look at life.

There is often and there must continue to be a distinction between that which an adult may see and that which a child should see. It would be even more valuable if there were a way of distinguishing between children and adults on the basis of a spiritual-emotional-mental maturity and not on the basis of chronological age alone. Obviously there is no such way, so for the time being we must either accept chronological age and draw restrictions on that basis or depend on the individuals and those who exercise control and responsibility over them to make the distinction.

Of course with all of this, the adult must not be thought invincible to anything by the very fact that he is an adult. There is a limit to the amount of sexual stimulation any psychologically normal person can take without response. There are certain things, if depicted onstage, which can make the audience guilty of a demeaning *voyeurism*, which can incite them to acts of immorality, and that can intrude upon the dramatic reality and destroy the integrity of the play. In a

May 16, 1959, editorial in *America* entitled "Candor Can Become Cancer," the editors had the following to say:

> Here is a film, let us say, which portrays in most explicit detail the intimacies of married life. In their proper setting and context—married life—such actions, far from being morally wrong, are ennobling and even sacred. But they would not be ennobling and sacred if engaged in by a married couple in the presence of guests in a living room. By what alchemy do they become ennobling and sacred when portrayed by a fictional husband and wife in the presence of thousands in a theatre?

Thus we see, at this point, that there must be two lines drawn after we decide in principle that sexual subjects are not *per se* objectionable. These lines are the general level of acceptability for all and the limit of acceptability for the young and immature. The whole matter now becomes a question of how and where the line should be drawn and who shall draw it.

As for the matter of "who" it should be, I think a basic principle is that the final decision must lie in the discretion of the individual involved or, with a child, in the discretion of the person who has moral responsibility for the child. No critic, no moralist, no artist, nor any other person for that matter, can make the decision for another. The critic, the moralist, the artist, may set forth the principle but the individual conscience is sacrosanct and no one can be the conscience of another. Surely there are times when we would like to avoid the proddings of our consciences and pass the responsibility to another, but this we may not do. The conscience is that one personal part of us where no other may set foot. Fraternal correction, yes, but the individual conscience is inviolate and no critic, no moralist, or artist may usurp its function. Consequent to this freedom is, of course, an obligation to inform ourselves about the particular moral question so that the conscience will not act blindly.

It is unfortunate but true that the Catholic public has become a watchdog, intent on sniffing out any signs of "moral laxity" or liberalism in their own Catholic reviewers and most of these are themselves busily engaged in the tiring and discouraging attempt to keep out ahead of the pack baying louder than all the rest. The pressure makes many of these re-viewers forsake the critical function entirely and they become like the vociferous "pharisees" that keep the pressure on with the letters of indictment that the theatre itself will no longer listen to. As they become like this "lunatic fringe" who seek to be more Catholic than the Church, the theatre refuses too to listen to them and they are rendered incapable of positive influence. They too join the futile Quixotic search for the "terrible Dragon, Sex" while meanwhile we are being eaten alive by ants.

Chapter Eleven

An Enema for the People

Thoughts on Tragedy for Today

TRAGEDY is ideally an optimistic thing. It shows man triumphing over adversity—achieving moral victory over the most cruel fate. It speaks out triumphantly for man, the noblest of God's corporeal creations who can fall to death, exile, dissolution, and yet manage to retain his human dignity in the full realization of his fate. King Lear is vastly more human and thus admirable in his final tragedy when he cradles Cordelia's poor dear corpse in his arms than he is as the testy old monarch of the early scenes. Hamlet is vastly more noble as he dies than he is as the young university man arrived home in the opening scenes. Tragedy refines and ennobles and thus it is, almost every time we pick up a learned magazine or journal, someone is again attacking the windmill of modern tragedy. We moderns seem intent on looking for our lost catharsis—that venerable physic of the spirit.

It's rather likely that almost everyone has seen an article or two dealing with the "problem of writing contemporary tragedy." Few read such articles, but for those few that do, it's altogether likely that the article was written by Arthur Miller.

In the accents of ordinary speech, in the idiom of the mundane, the conventional, the everyday, Arthur Miller has pitted his not inconsequential talents as a playwright against the difficult, if not absolutely impossible, problem of fashioning a tragic hero out of the common clay of contemporary man. With Death of A Salesman many thought he had achieved that self-set goal and largely as a result of that play, having never really found a true success since, Miller attained something close to first rank status among American playwrights.

Arthur Miller is, in a certain sense, Henrik Ibsen warmed over for a contemporary audience. Like O'Neill, he would be a new Sophocles and like O'Neill he falls markedly short. There is too much of Ibsen in him—too much thundering, too much the pointed contemporary image, too much the topical issue. Though Miller's aseptic language has a bite that

O'Neill could never have matched, it is in his didacticism, his moralizing, his constant reiteration, and his choice of character that Miller falls short. Most of these things we might forgive and it's just possible that Miller might be the one to write a contemporary tragedy, if it can be done at all in this day when we worship commonness. The common man and the tragic hero are truly contradictions in terms and we can hardly blame Miller for missing the unattainable, for failing to achieve the unachievable.

O'Neill was not so burdened with "the cult of the common man." Though Lincoln had already uttered his famous monstrosity about the Lord liking the common folk, the idea had not yet fully caught on and the process of cultural democratization had not spread *quite* so far from the Jeffersonian ideal. O'Neill's life, singular as it was, mingling with a certain aristocracy of poverty, vice, and drunkenness, could hardly match the "common man" influence of Miller's native Brooklyn.

O'Neill deliberately courted the remarkable, the dramatically unusual, and in doing so came at least thematically close in size and scope to the heroic dimensions of tragedy. Miller, from New York City, part of a self-consciously proletarian culture, turned his attention to the ordinary man living the ordinary life and lost immediately that which he had tried to capture even before the attempt was made.

Society will accept with no hesitation the sufferings of one of its rank and file members. There is no "catharsis" to use the technical, Aristotelian term, in seeing one's equal suffer. We are a bit relieved that we are not the victim and then we mutter, "What is all this to me? I'm sorry for the guy, but what can I do?" We say it not without callousness and then we go away. It is only in the fall of one who means something to all of us—one whose fate ritualistically or even in fact touches us all that the full truth of tragedy can be driven home to us. I don't suppose it's any accident that the word "tragedy" is derived from *tragos*, the Greek word for goat. The tragic hero becomes the sacrificial goat for all of us. He suffers for all of us, for he is somehow linked to us—he is our "super alter-ego." In a redemptive way he is led to the slaughter for all of us.

How can a stupid, virtually will-less Willie Loman be our scapegoat? Who of us can let the wistful Willie represent us? Willie's only will is in his name. Willie the insensate slob who is to be pitied as a confused wretch, not as a proxy for man. Why, there isn't even a realization, on the part of Miller's poor hero, as to what has happened to him. He falls with all the perceptiveness of a stray animal being hit by a speeding bus. The tragic hero *must,* or so both tradition and taste would have it, assume the burden of his tragic fate with human dignity in order to achieve theatre of the truly classic dimension.

Hamlet restores justice to his native land and is willing to pay the price for it, whatever that price would have to be. Macbeth is willing to take the risk for the dangerous game he played, and stand up and fight, if for nothing else, at least for consistency's sake. Oedipus accepts his exile with the dignity of a redeemer which in fact he later becomes. Willie merely goes down blindly. He lives as a mole and so he dies. There is no human triumph here, only the morbidity of a purposeless life and the lingering stench of self-murder. This is not tragedy. The protagonist finds no measure of triumph and goes from weak and appealing to beaten and dead. This certainly cannot be the divine spark of the tragic muse. If it is, better then that it should be allowed to die out.

A View from the Bridge is another Miller attempt to create a modern tragedy. He creates for us in the dulling, spiritually deadening environment of the Brooklyn waterfront a character named Eddie Carbone, longshoreman. Eddie is generous, passionate, nominally Catholic, hard-working, a man who has, almost unknown to himself, become overly fond of his niece whom he has raised from early childhood.

Growing within the heart of Eddie Carbone is this incestuous attachment to the girl—an attachment so terrible in its implications that Eddie, an honest and decent fellow, can't even admit that it exists. He can't admit it to himself. It grows and grows, however, while the young girl responds quite healthily and glowingly to the love of a young man—an illegal immigrant who has taken shelter under the Carbone roof.

Gradually, with this most secret and shameful desire gnawing at his decent soul and wreaking havoc with his judgment, Eddie drags his own house down around his ears like a tortured Samson and dies miserably, the victim of a knife, in the dust of the street.

Obviously, Eddie has acted with something short of towering virtue. He has harbored passion in his heart—a passion that had no right to be. He has foully maligned the young man who loves his niece, he turns informer and betrays the boy and his impoverished brother to the immigration authorities, he treats his long-suffering wife wretchedly . . . he does all these things and they are wicked things. There's no denying his guilt. We cannot, however, say the play is bad because Eddie does these things or because the playwright takes note of these things.

The play does fail, however, in that it doesn't achieve the stature Miller himself seems so intent on its achieving. It again falls short of tragic stature as Eddie, with his last breath, cries, "Why?" Miller doesn't permit him to know—doesn't permit him a moment of final truth in which he sees the tangled skein of guilt running through his life. This is even more critical in the play's failure to reach tragic height than the matter of Eddie's stature. It, too, however, is a factor. Those who go to the theatre would not—and one need look at our audiences to see the truth of this—accept Eddie Carbone as an equal, much less a hero in whose fall they are involved. Despite the words of John Donne that "any man's death diminishes me," and despite the brotherhood theme in our literature and drama since Whitman, our audiences are reluctant to be any man's brother—particularly if he drinks beer, belches, unloads ships, crosses himself, and is named Eddie Carbone.

There is no question that Miller is a good playwright. He misses greatness, but he writes ever so well for a theatre which is distressingly short of great talent.

Oddly enough, the play which brings Miller closest to contemporary tragedy is the one he is most criticized for: *The Crucible*. A play—a good play, this is—is not a piece of political polemicism. Despite the fact that Miller wrote *The Cruci-ble* while still smarting from a subversion investigation in which he prominently figured, *The Crucible* is vastly more than a piece of public vengeance. It is a stunningly good play. Though it was most certainly the result of Miller's experience with Congress that the play got written in the first place, it need not be judged on the political level.

Perhaps in John Proctor, Miller's protagonist, there is not what one might really call a moral flaw, but there is a prior weakness that can stand in quite well for the classic "inner flaw." Furthermore, Proctor is an honest man, a man of honor and integrity who *knows* what he is dying for. Here's something vastly more refreshing than the dumb brute dying in the street or in his car—the man of integrity dying to safeguard his name. Proctor is, to be sure, the victim of circumstance, but his prior guilt in what should have been an unrelated matter brought him full face with the gallows. His death, because he *is* knowing and honorable, occasions much more empathy in the audience. It provokes compassion and to a certain extent we feel vitally concerned in the fate of Proctor.

The last mentioned play of Miller is a real sore spot for many Catholics. Whenever it is done, one is bound to hear rumblings. That peculiar Catholic minority which considers anti-Communism an even higher virtue than the love of God inevitably gets restive when one speaks about doing *The Crucible*. Apparently they feel that listening to Miller's ideas regarding the evils of witch-hunting in Puritan New England involves some sort of "Comsymp" activity today. If they choose to construe the activities of the Senate Investigating Committee which interrogated Miller as in the same category with the false tribunal which convicted Proctor, then I suppose they have that right. I don't feel that an analogy of that sort is either necessary or desirable for the proper appreciation of the play. The play is about people and the issues that one can draw from the play are drawn from the people involved. Surely *if*—and I repeat *if*—we should investigate, try, and punish people today for motives of personal revenge, then *The Crucible* might have some topical relevance, but it's the old case of, "if the collar fits . . ."

A second argument used to indict Miller, both in reference to *The Crucible* and his other works, is one almost too ludicrous for words. It would be totally laughable, if it were not so pitiful. There are those who feel that any word of praise for Miller—any dollar spent to support him by buying tickets or books—is a contribution to the further infection of world Communism. As a reviewer for a Catholic newspaper I have received letters—serious letters—signed by allegedly responsible men and women who have indicted me as "a tool of the Kremlin" for admitting to the talent of Arthur Miller. This, of course, is based on Miller's pleading the Fifth Amendment when asked if he had ever been a member of the Communist Party or any of its front organizations. It has always been my understanding that in this country a man is innocent until proven guilty.

Returning to the subject of tragedy and its feasibility in the modern theatre, one can see, I think, that tragedy is not in any sense impossible today any more than it was in the age of kings except for the fact that men today cannot agree that triumph can originate in suffering and death. In a materialistic age, how is it really possible to appreciate the moral victory of the martyr, the triumph of the redeemer, or the satisfaction of the dying reformer? The problem of achieving cathartic tragedy today is not so much a matter of not having kings, because, of course, we still have them after a fashion, but a matter of consensus. We can't achieve a philosophical consensus.

When you go to the theatre today and sit in a row of sixteen seats, it's quite likely that a whole spectrum of philosophical disagreement is represented in the very row in which you sit. Perhaps the people there can't formalize their belief and say precisely what it is they believe in—precisely what they think life is and what man is—but they disagree and no tragic playwright with a clear belief in the ability of man to rise above himself and the circumstances of his times can find anything approaching unanimity in a contemporary theatre.

To be sure, one can find a certain nostalgia for heroism in the face of incredible odds, but no *real* tragedy can shake an audience today. Humanistic pathos, yes—the matter of genuine tragedy, I think not.

The plays we do have can, most certainly, occasion a wonderful compassion, even in an age of materialism. For example, William Gibson's rather sloppily constructed but magnificently conceived drama *The Miracle Worker* can touch the heart. Based on a purely humanistic norm, it can, when properly played, work marvellous things in the soul and one triumphs with little Annie Sullivan as she brings a child into the world of conscious man. But she *does* triumph. When there is no triumph, something else must be substituted to make the work acceptable. In the plays of frustration and ineptitude—plays with which our stage abounds—the audience must be given something else to divert them. They won't accept *moral* triumph, but they will accept Chekhovian frustration providing you make it diverting enough in the telling.

To use another of Gibson's plays for an example, *Two For The Seesaw*, fast becoming a summer stock standard, is a perfect illustration. Gibson has created a small hell in this play. Inhabiting this miniature inferno, smouldering somewhere in the concrete desert of New York, live two of the lonely damned—a girl named Gittel and a man named Jerry Ryan.

Gittel Mosca is one who eternally gives and never receives. One whose generosity bursts forth impulsively and almost blindly, she is a bohemian of sorts, a would-be dancer, an ulcer sufferer, and one who bestows herself freely on any lonely lad who asks.

Jerry Ryan on the other hand is one who eternally leans on others. He is a taker rather than a giver. He is a lawyer from Omaha who has been estranged from his wife for more than a month. He lacks self-confidence and, more significantly, for the moment, he lacks a woman. Meeting Gittel, Jerry asks and receives.

Their affair is a haunted one—now idyllic, sometimes humorous, frequently poignant, always tormented with the knowledge that it is built upon sand. With her generous encouragement, the leaning man braces himself, and when she is laid low by a hemorrhage, he has to stand up and do something for another person for perhaps the first time. He realizes that he can be needed by someone else and that he is a man who has it within himself to help another. Though it is Gittel

143

who has given him this, he goes back to his wife, leaving the little bohemian stranded high and dry on the beach. Like Orpheus, Jerry Ryan must leave the underworld without looking back to see Eurydice, who sits alone facing the dark.

I suppose on a natural level there is hidden in this play— beneath the image of its facile sex talk, its ever recurring profanity, its flashing humor, its moments of truth and sadness —some kind of human truth. It may have a deep and almost spiritual theme. Perhaps it has something significant to impart about the impermanence of these tenderly sad meetings when two lost human beings carry on what is in polite circles called an affair. Perhaps it has something cynical to say about those who become the willing victims of those who lean on them. Perhaps it says something, in an oblique way, about the strength of the marital bond.

With all this supposition and despite all the possible meanings, whatever they may be, *Two For The Seesaw* is the melancholic tale of two who let themselves get caught up in a situation that violates the laws of God and the accepted ways of man. They do not triumph in any sense and Jerry Ryan's return to his mate is a lame sort of return at best. The characters are intense in their humanity, living frantically, and somehow very, very tortured and sad amid all the joking. It is at times amusing, and at times embarrassing to look into so personal a human problem.

Now why can we flock to see this sort of thing and pass the tragedy by? How can we accept a pathetic ending and turn our backs, most of us, that is, on the hero's demolition in the flames of moral victory? It's hard to say. It may be that we enjoy ourselves along the way. Gibson has written some very funny moments into *Seesaw* and the sex talk could prove titillating I suppose. It may be, too, that we are embarrassed by heroism. We feel it's out of place in our century, like a great conscience of sorts. Perhaps it's worse to have a suit of rusty armor in the closet than a skeleton.

At any rate, it seems we'll take enervating pathos, flaccid melancholy in place of tragedy. I suppose it's our loss. *Two For The Seesaw* is not a great play. It lacks the size, the scope, the real dimension for that. It is, however, an undeniably sin-

cere play which gives us the sight of two persons in a des-
perate struggle with the spiritual and emotional emptiness that
preoccupation with the merely physical can bring. Gittel and
Jerry, like all too many of our generation, just make physical
contact as they meet, they never truly find each other. This
is the small beer of our times. No more catharsis, just a
modest malt diarrhetic.

Chapter Twelve

Whatever Happened to Comedy?

WHEN your world becomes black and blue and you retreat into the corners of your life, feeling for all the world like the monkey in the schoolyard rhyme who chased his tail around the flagpole, there is nothing like a little comedy to prove to you that things might be considerably worse. As you roar at the lady who sat on the coconut-cream pie or at the discomfiture of Sganerelle or at Malvolio's humiliation at the hands of Sir Toby, there is a certain release of your own torrent of troubles onto the heads of these hapless ones. Just as the tragic figure assumes our burden in the rhythm of the tragedy with its sacrificial inevitability, the comic butt takes another human burden upon himself as he executes the comic pratfall.

For all the jollity of the comic form, however, comedy is one of the most truly serious things in this world and in its surgical "pessimism" lies most of its value and much of its appeal. While noble tragedy with its so-called cathartic action on the emotions cleanses one, so they tell us, of fear and pity, comedy, with an appeal to the mind rather than to the heart, shows us the stupidity of our earthly ways. In the failings of the common man we see more than a faint glimmer of our own imperfection. Dealing as it does with the folly of mankind, the comedy lays bare man's foolishness, ferocity, frivolousness, and the phoniness of so many of his human institutions. As a social corrective it helps us to see our own faults, both as individuals and in groups, and it provides us with a sort of "misery loves company" refreshment as we see other men struck down with the slapstick. We sit smiling from the relative safety of our theatre seat.

There is a need for laughter in this macabre age, but in the words of G. K. Chesterton, ". . . in a world where everything is ridiculous, nothing can be ridiculed. You cannot unmask a mask; when it is admittedly hollow as a mask. You cannot turn a thing upside down, if there is no theory about its being right side up. If life is really so formless that you cannot make head

149

nor tail of it, you cannot pull its tail; and you certainly cannot make it stand on its head." (*Eight Great Comedies*, Mentor Books).

Perhaps this is the problem of our theatre that is vastly more critical than our contemporary failure to write Aristotelian tragedy. We haven't been able to write comedy—something vastly more necessary to society's well-being. There have been an increasing number of theories heard lately concerning the demise of great comedy in our theatre. Since the last George S. Kaufman comedy left the boards a few years back, American stage humor has been restricted to the sex farces of George Axelrod, the specialized humor of Thurber, the work of an occasional European wit (usually too ironical for sentimental Americans), or the grand, but again specialized work of those who create revues for the Yiddish stage.

Now and then we find flashes of comic brilliance in plays that are not essentially comic, as for example, in Paddy Chayefsky's *The Tenth Man*, but for the most part, great comedy has disappeared from our stage and no one seems to know why.

Great comedy is the result of keen observation of the world. The comic writer, a sharp and perceptive man who stands on the sidelines and views the staggering gyrations of mankind, records in his detached and facile manner the errors of humanity. He sees all the silly, preposterous, utterly absurd things that his fellow man does. He takes note of the countless deviations from the norm in the lives of his colleagues in flesh. Not, in truth, feeling anything for them but a careful objectivity, he dispassionately compares them with what they ought to be. The writer who pictures a fat-bottomed friar solemnly peddling an English bicycle, who depicts an irate political leader paddling a baby's behind rather than kissing its cherubic face, or who visualizes for his readers the glorious absurdity of a garbage man in white tie and tails, is observing the violation of a standard—the shattering of an expected pattern of human action.

Today, our human society is a fragmented thing. Dwelling in an age of self-centeredness, our eyes are turned inward and every man has attempted to make of himself a social and ideological island. Though we conform blindly to hollow mores and obsolete social usages, we cry out for individual interpretation of nearly everything else, and even those of us who follow a faith, who subscribe to a set philosophy, or who vote consistently with one political party, hear ourselves— our own voices—speaking out from time to time in terms of relative truth. Rather than right reason we are guided by sentiment and often our religious orientation, our philosophy of life, our political affiliations, become a matter of "team spirit" or mass psychology rather than a matter of earnest conviction. With the playwright Luigi Pirandello, father of a whole school of artistic relativists, we say, "Right you are, if you think you are!"

Our forefathers in theocratic Greece, in medieval Europe, in Elizabethan England, knew how to laugh, for they had before them in the ideals and attitudes of their societies a requisite for true comedy. With a sense of order, a knowledge of the nature of things—a knowledge that all society shared— they could see clearly the incongruity of man's deviations from the norms and natural laws of a sensible universe. Human nature was a known thing, subject to the laws of God and the "ground rules" of his creation.

Today, every man sets himself up as a prophet, subject to his own rules of behavior. Fortunately there is some semblance of respect for law and order persisting, though there are indications that the evident breakdown of the family and the softening of paternal authority in our society, even this regard is beginning to fade. If there are no generally held social norms, then there can be no great comedy. The break *from* the norm has no meaning unless there is a commonly held norm from which to break. This is the axiom of both human culture and the historical patterns of art. It is also common sense.

Another factor that holds our theatre back from the heights of comic fulfillment is the element of fear. Man is too frightened today with all the world's unrest really to laugh with heartiness. One must remain rather unemotional about something to enjoy real laughter at its expense. When a loved one, your father, let's say, falls flat on his face in a mud puddle after having meticulously prepared himself for a fancy dress ball, our laughter fades when we realize who it is and that he may have hurt himself. Even the comedian, like Chaplin, or more recently, Jackie Gleason, who sees fit to flirt with pathos, must hide his real humanity behind certain stereotyped symbols like the strange walk, the Hitlerian moustache, and the trademark bowler, in order to keep us from experiencing an excess of emotional identification which would immediately banish mirth from the scene.

With the ever present fears of contemporary life gnawing at us, it is difficult to become detached enough even for the initial guffaw. The great problems of the century are too grim for our laughter. With the absurdity of these cruel times, the chortle of amusement sounds too much like "the death rattle," and so our prophets of the absurd, Camus, Sartre, Dueren-matt and all the rest, see absurdity from the position of "en-gagement" rather than that of comic detachment. Thus comedy dies as we allow our small fears to mushroom into great ones.

For example, no one is writing quality comedy about the spectre of atomic war, the race problem, the withering of the family, and the threat of economic and ideological takeover by the Soviet Union. We are far too worried about these things and we have allowed too many of them—these troubles we exist with from day to day—to progress to the brink of disaster. The Romans, in the decadent autumnal days of their Empire, did not write comedy about the threat of barbarian in-vasion and how ill-equipped they were to face so frightening an eventuality. Instead they chatted about sex and social usages in their theatres. They did not direct the comic barrage to point up their weaknesses in the hope of transmuting them into strengths. They were a people who had fallen in love with their own infirmities. And so Rome fell!

Like the Romans, we follow suit: We produce our tedious sex jokes; our little joshings of earnestness and sincerity wherever and whenever we find them, and now and then, on the threshold of panic, we write grim sociological tracts about the dangers of mass "genocide-by-the-bomb" or other things equally cheery—serious warnings which do little to relieve the tension of the times or to rectify its problems.

The laughter of comedy is a social corrective. Many a grievous problem has been laughed away, for evil, based as it is on pride, cannot bear the stings of society's laughter. The comedies of Aristophanes and Molière, to cite but two of the greatest, lashed out at the evils of their day. Aristophanes tried with some measure of success (though who can measure the results of this sort of thing) to discredit the Sophists and some of the political demagogues of Athens. Molière sought to expose the charlatans of the then fraudulent medical profession, the hypocrisy of some of the churchmen at court, the *poseurs* and *dilettanti* of his society. They were not thanked for making these exposures, and they give evidence to the fact that the comic artist—one who would satirize the foibles of the world—must be made of heroic stuff. His targets are not only moving ones but they often fire back and usually their ammunition is physical or social punishment rather than a mere barrage of wit. Most of the great comic artists in the theatre—Gogol, Synge, Cervantes, Gay and others—were slandered and villified, if not subjected to worse treatment. Who is there now with the solid, generally accepted ideology *and* the courage to strike down the frauds and cheats of today?

With stringent libel laws and the extreme sensitivity of the great medias of publishing and the electronic media, it is all but impossible to stand up and expose the evils of society in anything but the most general way, for fear of treading on the toes of some influential fool. Only noted public bogeys like Señor Castro and Tovarich Khrushchev are legitimate goats. If we start striking too close to home with our comic brickbats, someone screams "foul" and the world starts battening down the hatches against us.

Our theatre today does laugh, but its laughter could better be characterized as a snicker than an honest roar of delight. It ridicules the staunchly honest, the intellectual, the chaste, and the peaceful. In the professional playscript, a girl who wants to stay chaste, the man who wishes to stay faithful to his wife, one who seeks knowledge for its own sweet sake, and one who bids for peace, are the butts and gulls of audience laughter. Of course we know that humor always had a talent for iconoclastic attack. The rich, the learned, the powerful, those who appear virtuous, have always provided targets for laughter down through the centuries. The Romans managed to attack the gods and the medieval Christian had many a good laugh at one saint or another. However, there is a *malaise* in our contemporary theatre in which good becomes the butt and evil the heroic quality *almost always*, as they are exposed to a shifting and, in a sense, ghostly standard of morality.

It's a sorry state of affairs with no immediate solution in view. It makes one think upon certain ominous historical parallels and precedents. The person who loses the ability to laugh at himself and the society which loses sight of its own foibles and failings are both riding for a fall. "Pride goeth before the fall," we are told. May we someday find our way back to a theatre that can laugh and say, "What fools we mortals be!"

Though we have lost the real comic sense—that of Aristophanes and Molière—the ability to detect absurdity has not been totally lost today. Though it has clearly passed out of the comic realm where it can inspire true laughter, there is a force somehow comic that can precipitate action from absurdity—from the serious contemplation of human irrationality.

Writers like the late Albert Camus and the remarkable Swiss novelist-playwright Freidrich Duerenmatt have manifested that they possess a clear vision of the world's absurdity —its deviation from its very own standards of humanity. Camus, rendering loathsome portraits of man's behavior toward his fellow man, shows a clear vision and a perceptive analysis of the horror that a lack of love or, at bottom, respect, can wreak. Duerenmatt with crystal-clear conception sees through a crawling mass of rationalization to the selfishness of what we humans too often call justice—self-interest. There is no question that these men perceive a standard and write with that standard in mind.

Their problem, like that of many other sincerely engaged writers of our times who revile the world in their writing, is the very vehemence with which they write. They become so enmeshed—so passionately involved—in the emotion of disgust that they often lead their audiences to the brink of hopelessness and despair. Does the work of Camus make us want to go out and rectify things or does it force us back to the lonely barricade of desperation? In the play *Caligula*, are the issues clear enough for us to know what to fight or are we so choked with his catalogue of moral horrors that our intellect refuses to act? We could wish that Camus had aimed his works deliberately at the comic effect rather than attempting tragedy, for the tradition of tragedy precludes action. Who walks away from Oedipus wanting to cure anything? Rather, one walks off saying, "Oedipus, despite his sin—despite the fact that he is but corrupt flesh—has won, through his pain, a moral victory and has saved his people. All is well with the world." By the passion of his *agon* he has saved us and we have been cleansed by his victory.

In comedy, the problem is quite different. We seek to cure the sores and boils that have formed on the susceptible flesh of history. This can be accomplished only by a *controlled* and *reasoned* disgust: a disgust that doesn't release the intellect from the problem of witnessing man and his actions in the theatre; a disgust that *involves* and yet does not excuse one from responsibility; a disgust of such a nature that it leaves room for hope and engenders a feeling within us that the wrongs can be and ultimately must be righted.

Bertolt Brecht, the strange genius of East Germany's *Berlinner Ensemble*, found the recipe for this therapeutic drama, this dark-masked comedy where absurdity is shown, where we are prompted to make corrections in the direction of our lives and our ideals. We see in his plays a world where man must sell himself in order to live—where he must not hesitate to drain his fellow man in order to sustain life. In the case of Brecht, the comic dynamism is put to use in the service of Marx—in the pursuit of the revolutionary paradise of economic, social, and political "pie in the sky." Brecht would essay to point out inconsistencies in our moral code based on your failure to conform and then send us from the theatre to revolt against our ideals, fashioning new ones more con-

formable to present expectations. For instance, in the conclud-
ing passages of *The Good Woman of Setzuan* the prescription
is "bigger, better gods or none." To be sure, Brecht is stacking
the cards against us, but he has at least found a way to use
humor significantly. He gives us the technical plan for a
theatre to serve as a social scourge.

Perhaps today there is something to be called "the black
mask of comedy." It may be that in our times we can find a
certain new dramatic dimension which can serve as a social
corrective—a leaven to bring forth this reasoned disgust of
which we speak so as to precipitate meaningful and effective
action.

It is indeed no accident that the ancient mask of "Arlec-
chino" is one of comedy's traditional symbols. It is a black,
ugly thing, patched with grotesque hair, and staring out at
life with an exacting, bestial intelligence. Comedy itself is a
basically pessimistic thing which shows us man, not as he
ought to be, but as he is—calced over with the lewd scales of
vice and wrapped in the hypocrisy of his fallen nature. In the
work of Boccaccio, in that of Rabelais, that of Chaucer, Swift,
Gogol, and Cervantes we see an image of the same poor fool-
ish man that was driven naked from Paradise, his flaccid
haunches lashed raw by the angel with the flaming sword.

Chapter Thirteen

God and Man—the Eternal Tension

THERE are indeed times when one begins to wonder if our present-day theatre will ever come to grips with God and the problem He presents to a materialistic age. To be sure we have seen a considerable number of attempts to "face up to the theological question" in the modern world and in modern society, but our theatre artists have been nearly as coy as our courts and our legislatures in using the name of God, except in something other than devotional phrases. Our theatre contentedly slithers around the periphery of heaven, making vague, non-denominational references to "the Deity" and slathering a few ethical problems about in order to pay lip service to godliness, but rarely, ever so rarely, does it face up to the gripping problem of man's relationship with his Creator. Somehow, in the theatre, as in government, it is thought to be embarrassing.

It is amazing that Paddy Chayefsky, a young *emigré* from the crass mediocrity of TV's living color "wasteland," should turn his talented hand to a drama dealing with the all-too-uncomfortable relationships between timeless God and temporal man in this era of spiritual estrangement.

Chayefsky, a prize-winning TV playwright, burst upon the public consciousness a few years back with *Marty*, a naturalistic piece about the loneliness of man's existence in the modern city. More recently he scored a brilliant success in the theatre with his *The Tenth Man*, a delightful play in which he stated his humanistic position—assumed his ethical stance —on the questions of love, spiritual restlessness, and modern materialism. In this play, told with both humor and profundity, Chayefsky dealt with the "dybbuk" inhabiting Twentieth Century man—the "dybbuk" of materialism and indifference. Still, however, there was no sign of the truly spiritual writer—the man who wrestles with God in the arena of his art.

The theatre has been, for as long as man can remember, a place for meeting ghosts, demons, beings on the supernatural order—a place of visions, dreams, and incantations. Macbeth's witches, old king Hamlet's ghost, the gods lowered from the *episkenion* in the Greek amphitheatre, Faust's Mephistopheles: all these have thrilled audiences back through the rich fabric of theatre history.

With Chayefsky's *The Tenth Man*, which had been originally titled *The Dybbuk from Woodhaven*, we had looked forward to adding a dybbuk to our string of supernatural acquaintances of the theatre.

Now a dybbuk is, in Hebraic mystical theology, a transient soul which migrates into the body of a victim as in the case of diabolical possession. Throughout the evening, Chayefsky's audience had been promised either a real live dybbuk or an exposure of fraud in this superbly acted, well-directed vehicle that runs, in typical Chayefsky blend, from startling melodrama to the most raucous of low comedy. At the moment of exorcism toward which the whole evening had been carefully built, and as the audience sat forward, expectant and lost in the magic of the Jewish ritual, Chayefsky chose to throw in the faces of his spectators a fistful of humanistic mush—a pinch of sentimental dust—a lot of verbal "hoopla" which suddenly threw an evening of solid playwriting completely out of focus.

The playwright should never admit cowardice. He should not fear to produce the demon he rendered necessary with the development of his plot. However, when all the rams' horns had sounded and the last prayer had been read, the playwright lacked the courage to write what he himself had led us to demand.

The Tenth Man is a play which attacks, at least on a practical level, the often discussed problems of contemporary Judaism. It places the old order alongside the new. It draws comparisons and makes accusations, as for example, the violent portrait of the crassly commercial, unbelieving young rabbi. It asks many of the questions and sets the stage for a showdown battle between orthodox religiosity, the mystical order, and the philosophies of despair and nihilism. Then with black candles lit, with scrolls exposed, with prayer shawls drawn over venerable heads, it fades away in an act of vague compromise

—a sort of ideological cowardice which makes much of the evening's enchantment lose its gleam in retrospect.

In *The Tenth Man,* Paddy Chayefsky missed writing a great religious drama by a hair's breadth. He missed by drawing back at the last minute.

Moving up to date, if Chayefsky's latest play *Gideon,* which tries to confront directly God—the traditional God of Chayefsky's Jewish heritage—turns out to be a failure, it will be one of the modern theatre's greatest failures—noble, grand in scope, audacious, and incredibly rich. It is terribly difficult to guess just what will happen to *Gideon* in the marketplace of the commercial theatre, for our audiences have not yet fully accommodated themselves to either the thoughtful play or the ritualistic play and *Gideon* appears to be both. If it does fail, it will likely be a matter of too much thought and too much sensation.

Odd as it may seem, *Gideon* surfeits us with thought and ravishes us with sensation to the extent that we sit, so overwhelmed with the vastness of the concepts explored, the boldness of the presentation, the visual pageantry of the Tyrone Guthrie production, that we are too occupied with seeing and hearing and thinking to really feel, concerned and indeed overwhelmed as we are with the barbaric spectacle. We are, in a strange way, "used" by the playwright, "spent" by the whole process and so debilitated by the assault on sense and mind that we, the audience, find it difficult to bring any response to the social intercourse of the play.

Gideon tells us that it is a hard thing to love God. It complicates life terribly, this love of a supreme being. It imposes limitations, restrictions, and obligations that we in our fallen state long to chuck. The great mystic, St. Teresa of Avila, was said to have once reviled God for treating His friends so badly. This, too, is Gideon's complaint.

An angel of the Lord, reflecting, it is vaguely inferred, the "appearance" and manner of God the Creator, appears to Gideon, a remarkably simple farmer. The angel tells the hulking Gideon that he is to champion God's people against the invading Madianites. The poor slug of a man barely comprehends, and reminds God that he is but a poor fool of a farmer, thought little of by his family; a bungler, little more than a dumb beast of burden. He is firmly told that all this makes no difference and that he must lead God's people out of fear and bondage. With a childish bravado pleasantly alternated with a touching humility, Gideon lays down his crude farm tools and assumes the mantle of leadership.

Borne to victory on the strong arm of Yahweh, his God, Gideon becomes, as all leaders tend to become, a little disoriented—a little confused by success and the power given them over their fellow men. The inevitable happens. Gideon, now dissatisfied with his lot, tries to erect "a cult of man," tries to invest himself with a new significance. God and Gideon have a falling out and it is precisely at this point that the play *Gideon* ceases to be merely historical. It loses its identity as a period piece and becomes a very telling contemporary play dealing with the lot of modern Jewry and indeed that of modern man in general. It shows our contemporary estrangement from God. It shows poor fickle man flirting with all sorts of philosophy as he flounders about, having renounced his birthright.

Many will claim that *Gideon,* with its talk of the "divorce" between God and modern man, misleads in trying to dramatize the relationship between the human being and his Creator. They will vociferously maintain that the gulf playwright Chayefsky, director Guthrie, and designer David Hays put between God and man is not, in truth, there.

These critics must remind themselves that *Gideon* is an essentially Jewish play written by a contemporary Jew. For Chayefsky, as in the case of his character, Gideon, there is no God-man, Christ, to bridge the great chasm between heaven and earth. It is in these terms—in the dilemma of modern Israel, still waiting for its Messias—that *Gideon* strikes sparks from the flinty realities of the Old Testament.

Chayefsky discusses the great problem of modern Jewry which, bereft of the Messianic presence, has a difficult time holding its youth to the old ways. To the naturally anxious young Jew, mere humanism has tremendous appeal because the flinty God who obliterated the Madianites at Manassas is too remote, too Olympian and hard for those who inhabit our times. There *has* to be a point of approach. There has to be an intermediary. The young Jew of our generation looks up in awe at the looming figure of Yahweh and says with Gideon, "Man must have more meaning than this." Christ invests man with this meaning by *becoming* man. The Jew has no such consolation.

In the play, the character of "the angel" (particularly as played by Frederic March) seems to have stepped from a William Blake engraving. Visually he provides a startling vision of God the Father though it would seem that the omnipotent God of Moses, Abraham, and Jacob shouldn't fret or whine or hide His face in petulant frustration when Gideon says that he loves Him no more.

The initial production of *Gideon* is important for reasons that go beyond the play and its authorship. Director Tyrone Guthrie, who was engaged by producers Arthur Cantor and Fred Coe, makes a significant contribution to the work and brings up another most interesting aspect of this challenging play. Guthrie, who has written most eloquently and aptly that the purpose of the theatre is to show man to himself so that he may see God in whose image and likeness he is created, builds a telling ritual for the terrible and prophetic divorce of Gideon from his God.

The work of Doctor Guthrie on *Gideon* is particularly significant in that we see, perhaps for the first time in the American professional theatre, a first-rank theatrical ritualist working with a basically "epic" approach in the theatre. The so called "epic" theatre (which seems irrevocably linked to the caustic works of East Germany's Bertolt Brecht), rather slowly catching on here in America, is concerned with the theatre as an instrument for the dissemination of ideas—for the propagation of an ideology. Though it was born with the Marxist socialism of Alfons Paquet and Erwin Piscator in the twenties, it is more a method—an anti-Aristotelian method— of drama than the tool of any one specific point of view.

Gideon, in the writing, seems profoundly influenced by the "epic" style, seeking argument rather than emotional response. There is a measure of the "epic" theatre's much-talked-of "alienation effect" running through it. To demonstrate this, whenever we begin to empathize too keenly with either Gideon or God, Chayefsky accurately and purposefully "alienates" us with humor or some common, dry observation and we are drawn back to the theatricality of the work, reminded in effect that the theatre is a lecture hall, a podium for debate. He reminds us that we are in a theatre being exposed to what is basically an argumentation rather than a play.

Another striking example of this is to be found in the closing lines of the play when the actor playing the god Yahweh steps down to the footlights to point out that God is no longer surprised to discover that man does not love Him. He speaks of the ruptured relationship—of the great tension of mankind's divorce from his maker—and then he leaves the inference, hanging in mid-air, that "someday man may . . . with this conceit we end the play!"

Chayefsky has here too manifested something of the "epic" influence on his work with an equivocal ending similar to that found in Brecht's *The Good Woman of Setszuan* in which an actor addresses the audience with a speech asking whether we should have "bigger, better gods or—none?" and continues:

> *There must, there must, be some end that would fit.*
> *Ladies and gentlemen, help us look for it!*

Like Brecht, Chayefsky seems intent on sending his audience out of the playhouse chewing on an idea, trying to resolve a question.

Now, in reference to Tyrone Guthrie, an exciting "new" dimension is added to Chayefsky's "epic" influenced writing and to Hay's "epic" setting. Guthrie, who makes of every play a ritual—who conceives the drama as a sort of earthy liturgy—has invested the cut-and-dried, matter-of-factness of the debate technique with the evocative panoply that has become his directional stock in trade.

Guthrie has demonstrated (how convincingly, remains yet to be seen) that the new disguise of "message drama" can be reconciled with the rich pageantry of traditional theatre *without* the emotional purge that theorists have deemed necessary for exalted and noble drama.

One might really say that in *Gideon* the remarkable conjunction of talents that created the fine, but relatively ortho-

164

dox *The Tenth Man* are evolving a "new" approach to the drama of religious tension. As they proceed toward this in *Gideon*, it must be noted that the approach is almost comic in nature. Unlike the dour "Calvinistic humanism" (if we can combine two such disparate terms) of MacLeish's frightfully overrated *J.B.*, the Judaic humanism of Chayefsky recognizes the God-challenging posture of puny man as essentially funny. Man standing on this shifting earth, threatening God with his disbelief is one of the more ludicrous things the human mind can dream up. This derivation of amusement from man is not shocking when one considers the approach of the medieval drama to the man-God relationship. In fact, the amusement is downright refreshing.

Again, we might point out that *Gideon*, despite the raves of the critics, is not the show to bet on. Audacity and invention do not necessarily pay off in the theatre. Audiences, reflecting eternally conservative man, are not eager to flock to the colors of the experimentalist. Chayefsky, honing the keen tools of his craft, whether he realizes it or not, is an experimentalist with *Gideon*. We might even consider him a sort of flat-footed visionary running at the head of the contemporary pack—at least here in the United States where experiment and improvisation normally give way to a sort of addled commerical expediency.

Additionally, with *Gideon* we are introduced to questions calculated to make a good portion of the audience uncomfortable. This, too, creates a problem for *Gideon's* brave producers. The audience of today, like audiences down through the exciting history of the theatre, are reluctant to *think* in the theatre—to *feel* is much more fun. The only consolation the producers can be sure of—for the success of *Gideon* is by no means assured—is to reflect on what the greengrocer may have said to the cobbler the night that *The Tragical History of Doctor Faustus* opened at Henslowe's Rose, "It's powerful, it's got a lot to say, but hell, I go to the theatre to be entertained. It'll never make the grade!" So may it be with *Gideon*.

Now, Chayefsky isn't the only contemporary playwright to tackle this theme head-on. The dilemma of reconciling man's ways to the ways of his Creator is a remarkably absorbing one and though there is a terrible reluctance to face up to it in the American commercial theatre, there are always a handful of candidates. I suppose it's the American equivalent to the French playwright's *bar mitzvah*, which consists of adapting a classical theme to the modern stage. It seems that then and only then is the French playwright ready to be seriously considered as a dramatist.

Perhaps of all the attempts at a drama of the "God-man tension," the biggest fuss was made over Archibald MacLeish's *J.B.* News magazines did features on it. Various eminent theologians argued about its implications, the critics wrote kindly of it, and the New York bartenders in the neighborhood of the ANTA Theatre touted it as the play which did the most to fill their bars after the intermission.

J.B. is based quite frankly on the Book of Job and considers the problem of human suffering and the question of why God allows us to endure agonies in life.

Clad in the theatrical framework of a travelling circus, with a balloon seller playing God and a popcorn salesman as the devil, *J.B.* attempts to show the condition of suffering man in the tanbark ring of a circus tent. J.B. suffers the loss of his children, the ruination of his fortune, the abandonment of his wife and the torment of pustulant sores outside and the horror of loneliness within.

Trial upon trial afflicts him as the devil prods and God permits, till at last, in a plethora of humanistic hogwash, he finds the answer to all in man—in his own human condition. *J.B.* just never gets off the ground, limiting his questioning to this world and accepting its answer in worldly terms. One wonders just what an earthbound "religious" play really is.

Mr. MacLeish, though he speaks of the God-man tension, has not, contrary to many eminent opinions, written a Christian play, though it is undoubtedly religious in a manner of speaking. The Christian seeks to find resolutions to ultimate questions outside the ken of this world—beyond the long fences of time—and finds the answer to suffering in an infinity far beyond the halting reach of a finite world. The play admits of no such answer, but must take its rawly unhealed resolution in time and so we have J.B. talking fatuously of "blowing on the embers of the human heart" and of starting again.

As for the entertainment values in *J.B.*, though each audience at the outset of the evening anticipates a theatrical treat as it stares into the wild promise of the Boris Aaronson setting, the play itself quickly dissipates any such hopes. For the most part it generates all the warmth and excitement of a non-denominational funeral.

Aide from the fact that we Christians cannot accept MacLeish's answer, if we can call it one, there is something about his cold crystalline poetry that stands in the way of *J.B.* as a piece for the theatre.

Certainly it is interesting verse and often arresting in its strength and almost classical severity. It makes far better reading material than theatre. Despite the torrent of torment that falls upon the drooping shoulders and bent back of the patient J.B., one can neatly avoid concern and stay purely spectator, for in the antiseptic world of MacLeish's precise and ordered imagery there is little room for warmth.

We hear love mentioned. We hear talk of warmth and all the beautiful things that are human. We are told of the poignancy of losing a loved one but it is always in the measured cadence of a clear, hard, disciplined verse. Never once do we see in the cardboard figures, with their set faces and cardboard words, the image of humanity. Never once does MacLeish show us anything but precise stereotype and never once does he show us that there is a God behind the ostentatious mask.

Both men have failed to produce an answer to the ancient dilemma. MacLeish has cheated and provided a "broken back" ending much as Chayefsky did earlier in *The Tenth Man*. In *Gideon*, however, Chayefsky proves himself man enough to see the dilemma. He acknowledges the problem and then tosses it to us. Instead of pretending an answer, unworthy of the initial concept, Chayefsky recognizes the sophistication of his audience and lets them in on the problem. After all, the theatre can only raise problems; it is up to the people to solve them.

Chapter Fourteen

Taking the Temperature of a Sick World

The Spirituality of Federico Fellini—

WHEN *La Dolce Vita,* the much-talked-of film creation of Italy's Federico Fellini, arrived in the United States, it had chalked up a most impressive record in Europe. Playing to unprecedented audiences on the Continent, this modern treatment of St. John's Apocalypse had already earned twenty-six important film awards. Since its initial release in February of 1959, it has caused a fantastic furor in Italy and elsewhere as people try to prove Fellini a pornographer or prophet—muckraker or moralist.

Fellini, previously well known as one of Italy's most accomplished neo-realistic directors, has been discussed on the international scene along with such modern greats as René Clement, Satyajit Ray, David Lean, Ingmar Bergman, Georges Clouzout, and Roberto Rossellini. He has furthermore become very much a topic of conversation here since *La Dolce Vita* opened in New York, April 17, 1961, at the Henry Miller Theatre. His work has intrigued many, bored many, and made a goodly number indignant with its "shock therapy" treatment for modern society. Fellini has proposed, in this marathon treatment of the excesses and aberrations of our times, certain questions that are downright embarrassing to citizens of the Twentieth Century. Fellini, who has said, "I think it is immoral (in a true sense of the word) to tell a story that has a conclusion," has created an episodic three-hour dilemma in celluloid which sounds the depths of modern man's spiritual degradation.

Federico Fellini is very much a child of our times. Born in Rimini on January 20, 1920, he came to Rome alone and hungry at sixteen, with, as he put it, ". . . no job, no idea of what I wanted to do." Adrift in a new and bewildering environment he first became a reporter, aimlessly choosing the fourth estate because, "I liked the coats they wore and the way they wore their hats on the back of their heads." He covered minor stories, the police beat, the hospitals and morgues. He took up radio writing and acting. For a time he toured with a ragged little vaudeville troupe, acting and writing sketches. All of this was done with a sense of aimlessness, a driving, disoriented discontent.

Finally, after writing a few relatively worthless screen comedies in and around the early "Forties," Fellini was given his big opportunity in 1944 to collaborate on the great film *Open City* with Roberto Rossellini and Sergio Amidel. This writing task launched Fellini on his subsequent career as writer, producer, and director of the so-called neo-realistic school which seeks, as its proponents maintain, "to set the camera in front of reality, making no comment." Aligning himself with those who *called* themselves neo-realists despite the fact that his profound cinematographic commentary and inspired selectivity seems often to violate one of their cardinal principles, Fellini, with *I Vitelloni, La Strada,* and *Le Notti di Cabiria,* established for himself an international reputation which ultimately enabled him to raise the $1,600,000 needed to shoot and release *La Dolce Vita.*

As the pinnacle of Fellini's creativity up to the present time, *La Dolce Vita* traces with countless parallels to the Apocalypse of the New Testament, the dangerous decline (if indeed it can be so considered) in contemporary moral standards, a decline we are often told that has led contemporary man to the very brink of disaster.

In symbols of great power and pointedness he recreates the modern Babylon in which we live so as to enable us to see our own image spread before us on the wide black and white screen. Fashioned in seven principal parts, *La Dolce Vita* follows a young reporter for a Roman tabloid through seven erotic nights of feverish pleasure-seeking and seven harrowing dawns of self-revelation as he sinks deeper and deeper into the quicksand of sensualism and turns his back on whatever higher nature he may have had.

There is something in *La Dolce Vita* that brings back the idea so familiar from the retreat master's conference and the warnings of the confessor, that grace refused—unheeded over and over—may not be offered again, and that the man who consistently turns his back on the loving offers of God, may find himself plunging down the well-greased chute to hell.

In this sense, the protagonist, Marcello Rubini, is a sort of unwitting Faust. He makes no deal with a corporeal Mephistopheles, but in his torment of *ennui* he tries to stroll out into the broad acres of self-indulgence which the devil conjures up before our eyes like a mirage. He tries to taste all the infinite varieties that sin seems to offer, only to find that sin is a terribly limited thing—very narrow—chained as it is to pride. We see graphically through the eye of Fellini's imagination that evil can become a morbid and monotonous thing, like a dull abdominal ache that defies diagnosis.

Faust's damnation here is not a matter of flame and brimstone or of a traumatic dragging of the poor wretch into a gaping Hellmouth, but rather a Kafka-like failure to communicate with grace. Innocence, in the person of Paola, the young girl from the little restaurant, faces poor damned Marcello across a narrow strait of water and he cannot comprehend her message—her invitation to the clean, broad unsullied beaches behind her. He stands on the other part of the sand, near the spot where the great gelatinous monster from the deep has been dragged up to glower at the hung-over revellers so morbidly intent on discovering its sex. He stands there in the presence of corruption and he cannot fathom what innocence wants of him. Finally, with a dazed shrug he is led back into the Twentieth Century Inferno. Instead of crotchety devils with bat wings to lead him, this newday Faustus is conducted to perdition by the soft, clinging flesh of a tanned girl in a swim suit.

La Dolce Vita is filmed in the flat, overexposed manner of a newsreel. There is no shadowy poetry here. Fellini's technique is a procession of sharp, clear images speaking precisely and unromantically. There is little indulgence in the quasi-poetic romanticizing we have come to expect from American moviemakers with their unbridled sentimentality. Fellini is economical and quick. His work is stark and dour with its lack of ornament. He does not dwell on things that do not relate to his central theme. He is cold and harshly truthful. When the yielding white flesh and exotic images of night give way to the chill antisepsis of dawn, the matter-of-factness of the film strikes us like a blow. It jars. It glares. It returns us to the reality of life and it shows us that life cannot be managed and twisted for the avoidance of all pain and frustration. The piper is always standing grimly about, waiting to be paid.

In this respect, one might find a suggestion of *Devotio Moderne* in Fellini's gloomy view of man—a view somewhat in accord with *The Imitation of Christ*. There is, too, something of the acute consciousness of sin to be found in *The Spiritual Exercises* of St. Ignatius. It is not terribly surprising that Father Angelo Arpa, S.J., a theologian at the University of Genoa, was a prime defender of the movie after its controversial release in Italy. Like an Ignatian meditation, *La Dolce Vita* castigates contemporary man for his inability or unwillingness, whichever the case may be, to find himself, to orient himself in the presence of God. With a dour and completely uncompromising vision, Fellini sees man disoriented and part of a "soft and adulterous generation" in swift and tumultuous pursuit of hedonism rather than in pursuit of Christ. He looks on in frank disgust at the narcotic state in which man so often places himself with the morphine of sex and the cocaine of alcohol.

In the dramatic confrontations of Fellini, in the harsh mornings-after, man always comes off badly. He twists, he squirms, to evade that which the new light of day brings him in revelation. Each lesson unlearned, he turns back to Mammon and the signs become more and more obscure as grace is more and more ignored. Our man becomes lost and in the gloom of a spiritual world not so very different from that against which Thomas a Kempis reacted; man becomes lost—a stranger to himself and to God.

Fellini has said, and it is obvious enough in the texture of his work, that all his films are concerned with people looking for themselves. The characters of *La Dolce Vita* bear this out so terribly. Emma, Marcello's mistress, searches for love— for someone to need her—so that she may identify herself with the maternal being she believes herself to be. Sylvia,

the strange unconscious piece of female flesh, seeks the delights of childhood which she has not really outgrown.
Steiner, the idealistic dilettante, tries to find his own measure
in the reflection of the universe only to find himself nothing
—a miniscule creature lost in the great jungle of creation.

All of them—the nymphomaniacs, the whores, the pimps,
the shysters, the opportunists, the homosexuals, the voyeurs,
the thieves—are people fleeing headlong from a mystery. All
of them, shaken by the terrors of life with its imponderables,
are searching in the fleshpot for the human identity—the
sense of order—that man loses when he cuts himself off from
Christ and builds his life around his own image.

Fellini is not a Deist like many of those in the arts with
whom he has been compared, for though God does not intervene in the Sodom and Gomorrah of the film, he is surely
evident. In the much-talked-of opening sequence when we
see a great statue of Christ being borne over Rome by heli-
copter, there is an obvious, almost too obvious, inclusion of
God. He is also very much present when the bedraggled human caravan returns from the orgy at the old villa, lust spent,
sopping the dry crusts of desire in the ooze of frustration.
There in the light of dawn they meet a priest in white alb
and chasuble on the way to Mass with his young acolyte.
The two groups meet and stand in mute confrontation. It is
as though a party of Martians had stumbled across an earth
man. They look at each other with a complete lack of common ground. There seems no bridge between them. And
they move on. The comparison has been drawn and Fellini
with the relentless ability of the true artist who must learn to
butcher his own children, moves his lens on, dwelling no further on the telling image which has already made its point.

The God of *La Dolce Vita* is not an avenging God, but
rather a God who waits and lets depravity prove its own
punishment for those who would embrace it. The emptiness,
the spiritual desolation, and the desiccated futility of "the easy
life" is so terribly evident. Like the strawmen of T. S. Eliot,
the people of *La Dolce Vita* inhabit a denuded wasteland.
They are dry—terribly, terribly dry.

Although God himself is surely present, there is no evidence in Fellini's world that Divine Love exists. There is nothing of the regenerative nature of grace that spreads beneficently through the fabric of Paul Claudel's work. There is no such luxury here. And we see nothing of Bernanos' flood of grace. Again, this is a spiritually bare world the film's creator spreads before us. Fellini's work is a lean recital—a visual parade of graceless, overt evil. There is no bursting forth of love from pride's ashes as in Mauriac. There is no transmutation of evil's waste into good as in many writers of, for example, France's Catholic Renaissance, for Fellini has not yet found the spiritual philosopher's stone that can transmute a Thomas a Kempis into a St. Francis de Sales. His emphasis is on the terror of spiritual bastardy and never on the family of grace.

As for the prudential aspects of *La Dolce Vita,* the Legion of Decency, in what many consider to be a surprising display of "liberal thinking," has said, "In the cinematic development of this theme, the film-maker has made use of some highly sensational subject matter. These shocking scenes, however, are never exploited for sensual delight; on the contrary, their shock value is intended to generate a salutary recognition of evil as evil, of sin as sin."

The Legion seems quite correct and judicious in making this assumption of good faith on the part of the film-maker just as it does in following this with a warning that "the immature" and "the passive" may be spiritually endangered by the work. They do, however, seem to join Fellini in considering sin on a purely natural level in their analysis of the film. Rather than seeing sin in its full enormity as a fall from God's friendship, they accept Fellini's working definition of sin as a deviation from essential good to an apparent good which does not consider the full and true nature of man. To be sure, this is not a bad thing, but it does not seem to go nearly far enough.

Despite whatever its opponents would make of it, *La Dolce Vita* is a film possessing titanic force. It has the great energy of its volcanic director and in its yammering insistence—its deliberate and dulling repetition—it hammers home something we already know, much in the way that a good sermon restates and renews old and evident truths.

Our society is sick. Fellini deliberately sets out to shock us with a forceful and astringent reiteration of our own misfortunes. It is not the shock of seeing something we had not seen before, but the shock of a new awareness at being forced to look carefully at things taken for granted. The things which we skim over in the newspaper over our morning coffee are decadent horrors and not merely a fanciful form of voyeurism provided by thoughtful and imaginative newsmen.

In simple truth *La Dolce Vita* is confession literature transplanted in a visual medium. It is, however, confession literature with a point of view. Fellini is more moralist than neorealist in this case. He doesn't snicker at the funeral of virtue, but he mourns clearly for what might have been. Though some have bitterly criticized him for not "showing the way back," for not suggesting answers and solutions for the decadence he depicts, he is sensible enough and artist enough to leave that job to the clergymen, the psychiatrists, the judges of the world. As he puts it, "I take the temperature of a sick world." Too often the artist tries to prescribe when it is his function merely to diagnose. Fellini can never be accused of this.

One can only marvel at him who can, in an age when deception and fraud are looked upon as normal practices, say, "A man's film is like a naked man—nothing can be hidden. I must be truthful in my films."

Chapter Fifteen

Plays or Penances

Observations on the Religious Drama

For too many years, religious drama here in America has been confined for the most part to a very few professional productions of fairly dubious value, offered by producers making a sort of "burnt oblation" at the altars of public piety. The gesture, which may be equated with veneration for such symbols as Mother, the nation's flag, courtesy on the highway, etc., is made with all due reluctance in order to placate and please the forces of organized religion.

In order to cast a little bread on the waters (not without a fervent wish for its return, multiplied a hundredfold) the occasional theatre businessman, after a richly rewarding success or two, might ostentatiously open some inane, historically obscure religious extravaganza. After its pitiful demise, despite the sex goddess prominently cast in a featured role, our producer friend is then able to portray himself as having done his duty to the temple. Of course, as he does this, he manages to pick up a nice pocketful of ammunition for later damning the religious play as "N.G. Ticket Sales."

In addition, of course, the whole project is tax deductible and he's drawn a salary to go with his heartful of satisfaction.

At the other end of the theatrical spectrum, on the amateur level, we have suffered thousands of school pageants, ineptly written, haphazardly directed, half-heartedly acted, and lukewarmly received. All too often, attendance at a religious play has spelled penance and mortification of the flesh to some poor fellow who has been summarily hauled away from the TV just before the Friday night fights to attend some performance of a passion play in a drafty parish hall where little Swithin, the brat next door, is about to play Judas Iscariot.

Again and again we have seen good intention substituted for skill in religious plays and the contemporary audience (or that part of it still vaguely endowed with taste) is driven ever further from the magnificent ideals of religious theatre. All too often, that which rather smugly calls itself "God's theatre," is much like a madonna from a potato by some pious scullery maid . . . beautiful in its intention, but hardly edifying in its execution.

Since laughing throngs gathered in the streets of medieval cities to howl at the extravagances of Noah's tipsy wife, religious drama, even then short on artistic stature with its ragged technique, has been on a skid-slide to oblivion.

Today's equivalent of the "peasant or tradesman" will take his entertainment in the form of a decrepit old television film or at an odiferous sports arena in preference to that dirty bore, the theatre . . . particularly the religious theatre. In our times, to attend a religious play means you're either an ascetic, an indulgence seeker, one who doesn't know it's a religious play, or a relative. People find it inconceivable that a play dealing with God and man can be entertaining. There's a feeling—a conviction, really—that religion and joy are incompatible. As Catholics we need only point to Chaucer, Rabelais, St. Thomas More, and, in the contemporary world, G. K. Chesterton. The feeling, however, persists.

Somehow, we Catholics (and most of our fellow Christians in America, for that matter) have retained from our American Protestant culture a shade of dour solemnity. Something quite alien to our *own* tradition has crept into us to dull the bright coloration so characteristic of our medieval heritage.

Religious drama in the Age of Faith was warmly applauded by the mass audience not only because of the Christocentricity of medieval life, but also because the dramatist of this earlier age, unsophisticated and uncomplicated as he was, knew something of the formula for causing joy to leap and cavort upon the stage. The medieval dramatist recognized this essential humanity of his vulgar audience and played to that humanity with every bit of his skill, unrefined and imperfect though it might have been. He knew how to appeal to man's fleshly self even as he played for his spirit. This was no mean skill in itself.

In the pageant of the cooks and innkeepers given at Chester each year, *The Harrowing of Hell*, the anonymous playwright did not hesitate to append a short and rather irrelevant scene to the matter of Christ's descent into hell. In this scene is introduced a woman who gave bad diluted and adulterated beer to her tavern customers. Of course she is damned, to the delight of all the stout fellows in the audience who have ever gagged on a tankard of bad ale. Though the scene has virtually nothing to do with the rather apocryphal tale to which it is appended, there is something of a healthy Christian moral and a wholesomely robust pleasure to be found when we see going to eternal damnation a woman who says,

> And when I was a brewer long,
> With hops I made my ale strong;
> Ashes and herbs I blent among,
> And marred so good malt.
> Therefore I may my hands wring,
> Shake my cans and cups ring;
> Sorrowful may I sigh and sing,
> That ever so I dealt.
>
> Taverners, tapsters of this city
> Shall be promoted here by me
> For breaking statutes of this country,
> Hurting the commonweal;
> With all tipplers, tapsters that are cunning,
> Mispending much malt, brewing so thin,
> Selling small cups, money to win,
> Against all truth to deal.

And so she continues, heaping invective and threats of hell on those who would presume to sell bad liquor and inferior beer. The scene is a funny one and well suited to appeal to every good drinker in the house.

Even the angels were not exempt from the spirit of fun that spilled over the edges of pageant wagon stages that brought the play to the populace. In *The Second Shepherd's Play* the shepherds do not appear terribly impressed by the angel who comes to them with the great tidings of joy, but rather they comment upon his singing voice, inferring rather openly that they can do as well.

We recognize that man is a union of body and soul. He is not composed of spirit alone. He has sense, tastes, imagination, appetites good and less good. The medieval deviser of plays sought the *whole* man and the *total* involvement of the spectator in the truly social bond of theatre.

These writers sought to address an audience of men, not spirits. They sought to translate into genuine everyday experience the scriptural history of God's people. They gave blood and substance in artistic form to the God-man confrontal in human history. They were cognizant of the fact that man, still clothed in flesh, learns through his senses.

Above all, these playwrights sought to contemporize the material with which they worked. They brought Joseph of Arimathea, Pontius Pilate, and the apostles themselves into their own *milieu*. They made Noah an object of sympathetic understanding by endowing him with a shrew of a wife.

Rather than whining some obscure approximation of a Judean dialect, their Noah swore merrily by St. John and spoke of "sweet Christ." The audience found mirrored on the gaily caparisoned platforms a reflection of their own lives in the happenings of ten centuries before. They heard their neighbors in the accent of angels and Roman soldiers, and in the profound utterances of saint and prophet they heard the voice of a God of their times—a God who spoke in language they could understand of things that concerned their daily existence.

They found the common, the mundane, the truly human problems of their own lives and times reflected in the art of the stage which seemed to reflect creation like the very cathedrals wherein the religious plays had formerly been enacted.

Today the cathedrals which were once painted and gilded in the brave, bold colors of God's spectrum are clothed in sombre grey. We seem to prefer them that way. We seek the monochromatic, the dour, the militantly joyless in our religious culture. We have lost both the impact of universal joy and the force of contemporaneousness in our religious plays.

What is the state of our religious drama? Do we see St. Joseph clad in the overalls of his carpenter's trade, feeling the weight of problems much like ours on his broad shoulders, or do we see an effeminate grouch in strange robes, holding a lily in one hand and a flimsy carpenter's square like a cocktail napkin in the other? Do we hear in his voice the rough, honest tones of a tradesman-artisan or do we hear something un-reconcilable and distant like the voice of God in a Cecil B. de Mille movie? After all, the saint has passed from time to eternity and thus belongs to all ages. The gilded icon of another time and place has little to say on a stage whose art is "the art of the immediate."

At this point, however, one may argue that the theatre is not for moralizing and therefore who cares whether or not we empathize with Saint Joseph. The theatre is a place for entertainment, for thrills, for beauty. Even in the religious theatre, if drama is not to become "theatrical religion," the primacy of the recreative aspect must remain ever clear.

This business of "theatrical religion" is a matter that crops up whenever religion and theatre share the conversational arena for any time at all. A few years ago, I happened to attend a so-called religious drama workshop in Chicago at the American Educational Theatre Association. A sizeable group of people had gathered to hear a panel of "experts" speak on the subject of religious drama. These "experts" were college drama people with a strong background in lay church activity and for the next hour or so, we were regaled with a lot of very edifying talk about "the drama of Christian experience in the Church" and about "ordering the service to manifest religious truth in meaningful symbol," until one began to wonder whether the workshop had not somehow shifted to become a church conference trying to figure out how to put the theatre to work in the sanctuary.

After listening to these people talk for a time, the whole thing began to suggest a nostalgia for the lost liturgy (lost to the several religious groups represented on the panel) of the Roman Catholic Church and an effort to fatten up the lean liturgy of the Protestant service with some poetic pageantry. This can hardly be called religious drama. There is little question here of putting religion into the theatre. It is rather, for these folk, a matter of getting the theatre inside the church. Catholicism needs no such liturgical embellishment and for us, in seeking our "religious drama," the orientation must be quite different. What we are seeking is depiction in terms of human action on a stage, something of the great excitement and the terrible wonder of man's wrestling with God in the great problems of human life.

It is in *this* vital relationship that religious drama is to be found. It is not a matter of rendering a biblical story in chaste and highly metaphysical verse patterns and then putting it on in a sanctuary or the garth of some cloister-turned-museum. It is rather misleading to base a definition of religious drama on its location and the question of whether or not the story comes from Sripture. Our medieval brethren did not hesitate to move out of the churches nor did they hesitate to move away from strictly biblical plotting.

The modern concept of Catholic theatre traces back to France immediately after World War I when a dissolute Red Cross doctor named Henri Ghéon came back from the battlefield reconverted to the Catholic faith of his childhood. Ghéon, a companion of the often scandalous, genius-haunted Andre Gide, had come back to the faith with a burning desire to put his talents as a writer, drama critic, and artist (he was but a half-hearted doctor) to the service of Christ.

One day, having met illustrator Maurice Denis on the street, Ghéon was challenged by Denis' disgusted comments on the quality of the religious theatre to be found in schools and parishes. Denis commented, too, on some of the amateur groups that had been founded to popularize religious theatre in the face of the cabarets, the music halls, and the *theatre du boulevarde*. The painter asked Ghéon, who had achieved a modest success as a professional playwright and drama critic before the war, why he didn't turn his hand toward improving the Catholic theatre. Denis was supposed to have said, ". . . at any rate, your efforts should be somewhat less miserable."

For fifteen years, the mortal remains of Ghéon have been mouldering in the Dominican Fathers' cemetery at Montparnasse, but like the immortal Abolitionist of American history, John Brown, "his soul goes marching on."

I speak of Ghéon's soul in the sense of his inspiration today for those who would turn a hand to the business of religious drama.

Ghéon was a pioneer. Although religious drama was not

completely unknown in the world of the drama when the forty-year-old country doctor turned his hand to *théâtre chrétien*, there had been no really theocentric drama assaulting the world of the professional theatre for centuries. To be sure, in the France of the early Twentieth Century there had been a number of uncertain efforts to come up with a viable religious theatre, but these were largely amateur groups whose competence was vastly inferior to their sincerity and good intentions.

Upon Ghéon's decision to re-enter the craft of the theatre, it was reasonably easy for him to find production. Through his friendship with Jacques Copeau, with whom he, Gide, and others had founded *La Nouvelle Revue Français*, he was able to secure production of his *Le Pauvre sous l'escalier* which opened at Copeau's famous Théâtre de Vieux Colombier in 1921.

As Ghéon's nephew, François Corré said of this play,

> *Pour la premiere fois un auteur Français parle de*
> *Dieu sur une scène de théâtre et fait dire un priére.*

Ghéon attempted to bring Christ to the theatre and not to bring Dionysius into the church. All too often, in our discussions of religious drama, we become confused in regard to the primary aims it is meant to fulfill. Ghéon did not need or intend to bring a richness and beauty from the theatre into the sanctuary, for as a Catholic, he was heir to a meaningful and well-ordered system of rubrics which neither needs nor welcomes additional dramatic elements over and above the real life sacrifice of Calvary.

Ghéon attempted rather to express in dramatic terms the heroic relationship which exists between certain men and their God. He sought to place in telling theatrical terms the heroism of the saint. Ghéon treated constantly of the so-called "folly of the cross" in which great souls defy the apparent logic of the mundane world to devote themselves to God even in seeming disregard of their own well-being. In his *Le Pauvre sous l'escalier* we see St. Alexis who walks out on family security, a beautiful wife, his good name, wealth, everything . . . in order to become an unwashed cenobite dwelling humble and unrecognized beneath a stairway in his own home. In *Le Pendu dependu* we meet a pitiable moron who gains true wisdom and the reward of Lazarus by voluntarily accepting death in order to preserve his father from hanging. In *L'Épiphanie*, poverty is extolled as a superhighway to happiness and in *La Merveilleuse histoire de jeune Bernard de Menthon*, the hero walks out on the woman he loves to answer God's call.

As regards treatment, Ghéon chose to revive the pre-Reformation technique of juxtaposing elements of high hilarity and sublime religious exaltation—to superimpose solemnly moving incidents on a background of the homeliest earthiness. This mixed style was perhaps the major cause of the Paris critics' harshness toward most of his work. It was also, in large part, responsible for his enduring popularity among rural audiences and unsophisticated artisans in countries where his plays have been done with any degree of frequency.

Keeping these two points of approach in mind, it is interesting to compare the pioneer work of Ghéon to that of the several major religious dramatists who have since followed his example either by intent or accident. We can gain some understanding of our present state in the field of religious drama by comparing Ghéon's ground-breaking efforts with the subsequent efforts of Claudel and Obey in France; those of Fry, Eliot, Sayers, and Greene in England; those of Paul Vincent Carroll in Ireland; and those of Thornton Wilder and Archibald MacLeish in the United States.

To be sure, it would be easily possible to include several dozen playwrights from half a dozen nations, if this were a comparison of all religious playwrights of our times. We might even include Bertolt Brecht, mentioned in a previous chapter. Brecht's plays were often concerned with theological points, though his works could not be considered, in any sense, *théâtre chrétien*.

There is more than just a superficial kinship between Brecht and Ghéon in that each was attempting at times to put across an intellectual message and clothe in human form the abstractions of a *credo*. Both at times adopted similar means and borrowed heavily from the highly conventionalized theatre of the Orient.

Initially comparing Ghéon to his countrymen Claudel and

Obey we find out that our country doctor from Bray-sur-Seine lacks the sophistication of either of these other French dramatists. We do, however, find a Ghéonesque ring in Obey's great play *Noah*. The direct and forceful opening speech of Noah to God sounds as though it might have been written by Ghéon, particularly the fully mature Ghéon who wrote *Noël sur la place* in 1933. The almost frightening simplicity of man's relationship to God as stated by both playwrights suggests a bond of insight between them.

Francis Fergusson, in his *The Idea of a Theater*, calls *Noah* the product of "a theatrical folk tradition going back to secular medieval plays."

Ghéon turned often to this tradition in gathering material for his religious drama. At least fifteen times, he turned to such inspiration as he wrote some of his sixty-one religious plays. Andre Obey's talent for humanizing the biblical hero is shared fully by Ghéon and in this sense, in their ability to contemporize along with their medieval progenitors, we can draw a significant parallel between the two writers. On the other hand, there is a slick and carefully calculated air about Obey's works which makes them somewhat more acceptable to a coldly discerning commercial audience just as Ghéon's complete lack of sophistication would not. The childish Franciscan joy of Ghéon and his shining optimism are missing from the work of the sober craftsman Obey.

The work of the great diplomat-poet Paul Claudel must be mentioned when one talks of contemporary dramatists who deal with the God-man relationship. Claudel is generally thought of as one of the greatest religious dramatists in our times. The power of his poetry and the terrible violence of his themes make him most assuredly the Titan of the *théâtre chrétien*.

In comparing Henri Ghéon to Paul Claudel we must, however, realize that there is a great disparity between their abilities as poets, but though Claudel is master in this respect, it does not follow similarly that there is a like contrast between their abilities as dramatists. In examining two of Claudel's major works, *L'Annonce faite a Marie* and *Le Soulier de satin*, and holding them up to Ghéon's norm, we find that Claudel

wields a far less deft hand in managing the stage and its conventions. His plays are loose and rambling in construction
when compared to Ghéon's decidedly more modest and
tightly knit works. Comparison on this scale would be something like comparing a man who *tries* to carry an elephant and
a man who *succeeds* in carrying a dog. Claudel may have gotten the whole back end of the elephant off the ground, but
Ghéon carried the whole dog.

Claudel's staging at times defeats the purposes of all concerned, with its tremendous technical demands, whereas
Ghéon, with his vast experience in the theatre, keeps in mind
the elements of production. Ghéon is a master of theatricality
and Claudel is a master of poetic expression. Good religious
drama need not be poetry. There is sufficient poetry in the
contemplation of the relationship that exists between the character who embraces the "folly of the cross" and the God who
died on it.

As for the aims of the two men, we can also note a difference. Ghéon, as we have discussed, writes of the Christian
hero. He shows all the Christian virtues in his characters as an
example to all men. The characters of Claudel seem instead to
be attempts to prove that "God writes straight with crooked
lines," as an old Portuguese proverb states. This is the proverb
that Claudel is said to have repeated so often as a justification
for his tales of sin and evil in tangled lives. Rarely do Claudel's
characters hasten to embrace the cross as do Ghéon's. They
are instead driven to the cross by fire, battle, famine, plague,
or tempest.

It is likely that Claudel will always lead Ghéon significantly
in the matter of professional productions afforded his work. It
will also be true, however, that Ghéon will more readily be
done by the large number of little amateur groups that seek
modest, easily produced, yet good religious plays as grist for
their theatrical mill. The sophisticated man who has seen
nearly everything would rather see a man strain himself to
tilt up the back of an elephant than to see a man trot confidently across the stage with a Great Dane in his arms. The
simpler man would think the elephant tilter a damned fool and
the canine carrier an admirable fellow.

Another difference is perhaps the matter of Ghéon's simple language as contrasted to Claudel's rich evocations.

But despite these points of difference, there is an even more basic difference in the appeal of Ghéon and Claudel. We must face the fact that the sophisticated, "cultured" man cannot sit rooting for good, but would far rather be teased and titillated with evil as long as a good end results. Evil is far more enticing for dramatic material for the sophisticated social experience of professional theatre-going than good, for it gives far greater opportunity for conflict out of which exciting theatre is made. St. Augustine is better remembered for his sexual sins than his sanctity.

Moving across the English Channel we find another group of contemporary playwrights who may well be compared with Ghéon in order more fully to explore the place and significance of contemporary religious drama. Christopher Fry, T. S. Eliot, Dorothy Sayers, and Graham Greene are but a handful of the most outstanding examples of British interest in the religious stage.

Perhaps the greatest resemblance to Ghéon and to the medieval heritage may be found (in a style sense at least) in Sayers' *The Zeal of Thy House*. In this play, freely calling on theatrical convention, with a commenting chorus of archangels, Miss Sayers tells the story of William of Sens, an architect, and of the spirit of love that ultimately overpowers his pride. Freely mixing a human sort of comedy with the driving seriousness and throbbing sincerity of the play, the purgation of William is traced from the day he realizes God does not *need* him for His work.

Often breaking the frame of the narrative in order to comment on the doings of William and his monk employers, the playwright seems to borrow a great deal from the choral techniques of the Attic Theatre and yet there is a unique blending of *sublimitatis* and *humilitatis* harking back to the medieval drama. In this respect we can see a relationship of sorts between Ghéon and Sayers, for as we have noted, Ghéon received his ideas from many sources. The major difference seems to be Sayer's formality as opposed to Ghéon's almost childlike candor.

In general we can say of all four British playwrights mentioned in this chapter that none of them write with anything approaching the simplicity that we find so winning in Ghéon. Eliot with his impressive, erudite, and not very communicative verse drama; Fry with his wry word games and dancing flights of metaphysical fancy; and Greene with his psychological torture chambers for an assortment of wholly undistinguished contemporary characters, all share in something vastly more sophisticated than anything Ghéon has to offer. Eliot's searching for Divine paternity, Greene's probing for moral sterility, and Fry's bizarre journeys into semantic jungles, are of a vastly different cast than Ghéon's forthright statements of Christian code.

As to who writes best, it is difficult to say, for in regard to the genuinely popular audience (if indeed there is such a thing), none of the playwrights mentioned has really succeeded. All we can do is to take note that the approach is different and the object is different despite the fact that it is all basically religious drama.

Paul Vincent Carroll shares, it seems, *only* his religious faith with Ghéon, for with the exception of his fairly recent Broadway production, *The Wayward Saint,* he stays almost exclusively in the realistic presbytery parlor and deals out miracles with a niggardly hand. In the most famous of his plays, *Shadow and Substance*, he comes closest to essential Ghéonesque patterns when he exalts the humble Bridget to humble the self-exalting Canon Thomas Skerritt, thus hinting at Ghéon's "folly of the cross" theme.

Carroll's later play, *The Wayward Saint,* deals out miracles more lavishly and even comes up with a thinly disguised devil. It has a certain folk-type humor that might prove acceptable to the same type audience attracted by M. Ghéon—the unsophisticated. It is still to be seen whether *The Wayward Saint* represents an isolated experiment for Carroll or whether it represents a genuine new channel of art.

Finally, turning back to our side of the Atlantic . . . focusing our gaze upon our own playwrights, we come across Thornton Wilder, and recently entering the picture, Archibald MacLeish. "Stumble across" might express the manner of discovery better, for there is a vast gulf separating the universal Catholicism of Ghéon, Claudel, and Obey, the somewhat more parochial of Carroll, the high-churchiness of the British group (including Quaker Fry and Catholic Greene), from the rugged American Protestantism of Wilder and MacLeish. Nevertheless, here we may discover the closest parallel to Ghéon and it may well be that in our own American soil a real "Ghéonic seed" may ultimately take root. It may be that American playwrights and American audiences can do what Ghéon sought and did not have the substance to achieve—bring popular religious drama to America. In these men we do not see the typical British attempts to put the play between altar stone and communion rail—to bind it to the chancel—but rather men who, like Ghéon, write religious drama for the market place.

Wilder, for example, is not so much concerned, as are many of the British Drama League and certain members of the American Educational Theatre Association's committee of religious drama, with worship in dramatic terms, but with a theatrical expression that deals with existence in a God-created world that clearly shows His hand and His influence.

Both Wilder and Ghéon wrote frankly presentational plays that rely heavily on stage managers that step in and out of the illusionary framework of the play. Both writers at times banish scenery from the stage and force the audience to use imagination. There is a marked emphasis in the dramatic theorizing of both men on social theatre, with its close communion between author, actor, and audience. Both borrow heavily from all the sources of historical drama.

There is a relationship, too, in the way the two men are received by the audiences. The sophisticated theatre audience has a tendency to reject both Wilder and Ghéon, though Wilder has certainly gained recognition on the professional stage, whereas Ghéon has not. It must be remembered in this connection, however, that this country has no such tradition of rationalistic anticlericalism as has France, and Wilder is, of course, far less overtly religious in his work.

Thematically, there is a considerable difference between Catholic Ghéon and Protestant Wilder. Wilder does not have the objective religious symbols of Roman Catholicism available to him so must discover his own symbols such as George Antrobus, Grovers Corners, and the huge table of *The Long Christmas Dinner*. One might describe Antrobus as the saint of the humanist, Grovers Corners as an American style "City of God," and the table of the one-act play a secularized symbol of human history in the light of scriptural historicity. For the privilege of having ready-made images upon which to hang his ideas, Ghéon pays a price in personal prejudice which curtails his general acceptability.

In regard to MacLeish through his much-talked-of *J.B.*, we see more resemblance though *J.B.* is considerably more stark and Jansenistic in its tone than Ghéon could ever be. In the strong biblical theme, in the play-within-a-play device, in its presentational flavor, and in the contemporizing of its theme and main characters we find a number of resemblances both to Ghéon and to the medieval stage.

There are also conspicuous differences. Most apparent of these are *J.B.*'s lack of a strong resultory climax and the presence of long flights of poetic language. In Ghéon we find no such ambiguous resolutions and unanswered questions, and flights of poetic fancy are rare.

Obey with *Noah*, Claudel with a number of his major works, Fry with *A Sleep of Prisoners* and *The Firstborn* as well as some shorter pieces, Eliot with *Murder in the Cathedral*, *The Cocktail Party* and, to a lesser extent, with *The Confidential Clerk*, Wilder with *Our Town* and *Skin of Our Teeth*, and MacLeish with *J.B.* have all received a certain measure of acceptance on the professional stage with religious drama. More recently Greene's *Potting Shed* and Carroll's *The Wayward Saint* have at least found production. England's Robert Bolt has achieved great success in his native England with *A Man For All Seasons* as has John Osborne with his much argued about *Luther*. Jean Anouilh achieved great acclaim with the at least peripherally religious *Becket* and his countrymen Sartre and deMontherlent have turned again and again to religious problems. There are certainly signs that the seeds planted by the frustrated Ghéon are slowly bearing fruit though the man who planted them has been forgotten.

Chapter Sixteen

Parting Shots

IN THE preceding chapters, I have gone on discursively talking of things that interested me—striking things seen from my seat just off the aisle—things that may have some bearing on our theatre and our films and how we Catholics may affect and be affected by them. There are many more things one might talk about in looking at the modern theatre, for it is incredible in its variation, the variance of its many points of view, the contrasting means it employs to reach its audiences. However, I remember what my father used to say half-jokingly when I was a small boy,

"Don't spend all your money now. Leave some in the bank for 'seed.' "

It's not a bad idea and so some of the thoughts that have occurred to me in the last few years will remain unspoken, perhaps sprouting somewhere in the dark.

There are a few thoughts though—thoughts I couldn't fit into my format, loose as it is. And so here, gathered under the general title of "Parting Shots," I'll let fly.

First of all, if conflict makes for real drama—we are told by theorists and scholars that such is the case—then there is something of intense drama to be found in the dual nature of America's theatre businessmen. The men who make command decisions in the theatre, whether they are called producers or whether some other euphemism is employed to describe their function, are strangely schizophrenic in their approach to the ancient arts of the theatre. They supply the gawking world with the wonderment of a dilemma.

Beneath the slick business exterior of many a theatrical producer often lurks the heart of a romantic child, and for every success of the commercial pragmatist, there is some strange and frightful fiasco that makes one question whether the theatre has ever heard of such mundane things as economics, market research, and advertising. One wonders whether "hardheaded" as an adjective referring to Producer "X" merely refers to the coating and not the contents of the cranial cavity, as we are regaled with a succession of flips, flops, and near-misses helplessly floundering onstage, crowned every now and then with one of the infamous pre-production cancellations that beset us, the public, and drive box office managers to talk of extreme measures.

How can this happen? Every year we see it and nod sadly at the waste of it all; yet each new year brings a new turkey or a dozen of them thoroughly frozen and suitably unpalatable. The veneration accorded to the professional theatre and its practitioners begins to sound a bit tinny as we watch the progression of failure after failure giving the theatre the appearance of a stumbling drunk, down more often than he is up. There are some who see a certain romantic ideal in all this uncertainty and perhaps for these, the commercial misadventures of the theatre are its salvation in their eyes. To them, its fiscal vagaries are the vindication of the "art for art's sake" school of thought which would have the theatre living off the largess of a generous public.

For our tastes, this is hardly a realistic or historically valid point of view, for the great dramas of history have largely been the box-office successes. Molière did little of note in the theatre until a stay in jail for non-payment of debt taught him the financial facts of life, and Shakespeare was certainly commercial. The competition of bear-baiting, cock-fighting and other less-than-respectable pastimes available on his bank of the Thames required a good business head of him; he had just such an asset.

As a note of caution one might add here that there are extenuating factors behind some theatrical failures and one can hardly categorize "dollar flops" like *Take Me Along, The Andersonville Trial*, and *The Wall* with such utter, ill-conceived catastrophes as *How to Make a Man, Juniper and the Pagans, Hail the Conquering Hero*, and *High Fidelity*. These last are the enigmas. How so much money can be pumped into the veins of a business corpse is the eighth wonder of the modern world.

It is the subjective vision that fools us. To be sure, there's room for personal taste in the commercial temple of art, but it is the audience, that hydra-headed arbiter of taste that makes the truly valid judgement. Perhaps an act of faith in the ultimate good taste and common sense of the general audience might be in order—not the special coterie audience that we often take for the real thing, but the genuine audience of taste and vision that can, and from time to time does, inhabit our theatre. Perhaps a little market analysis might be in order.

As critical as this lack of judgement may be in some of our producers, it would be a matter of gross oversimplification if we were to consider the problems of our theatre only in terms of taste and judgement in the choice of scripts.

In this day when we have become accustomed to seeing giant actors on the motion picture screen—actors who are so magnified in physical stature that every gesture, flicker of facial expressiveness, change of objective, can be easily seen and immediately perceived—it is somewhat disturbing to find oneself dumped in the twenty-sixth row of a theatre.

The motion picture, bestowing upon us the vision of a man's hand holding a gun that measures ten or twelve feet in height, can certainly make the opera glass as outmoded as a slingshot on a Nike base. We are accustomed to large, easily-seen actors, and we enjoy the situation a great deal. No conventional theatre can offer us this degree of amplification, which is, in effect, getting close to the actor so that we may detect every nuance of his craft.

It is, in part, as an answer to this problem that arena stage was born. In seeking to bring people closer to the actor, closer to the action onstage, it was inevitable that the auditorium with its seats should be "wrapped around" the stage again so as to bring every audience member at least a few feet in toward that center of all theatrical interest, the living actor playing onstage.

It's obvious that we can't transform our commercial theatre overnight into arena playhouses. I'm not sure that it would be any more desirable than it is feasible. We can, however, seek to make the theatre more vital, closer to the audience, and more in keeping with the historical ideals of the theatre. There are many ways of doing this short of pure arena theatre and our theatre visionaries might well give some attention to this point as they search for areas of activity—areas where genius and imagination are needed. It's similarly obvious that this is just one of the many more or less technical problems in the total picture.

There are many other challenges besetting the modern theatre and it should be clear to anyone who reads that they are being well considered in the press, in magazines, and by those who write books. Barely a week goes by when someone doesn't analyze what's wrong with the theatre. There is little I can hope to add in this regard except to call attention to one point—one question that has been somewhat avoided in all the chatter about everything ranging from theatre economics through the concept of "glamor" on down to the chalky taste of the insipid orange drink in the lobby.

If a man fighting for his life against a fierce tiger were to refuse a ceremonial sword because he felt that by blooding it he would somehow sully the honor of the blade, we would wonder about his sanity. As this man went down for the last time before the slashing fangs of the beast, at least some of us would say, "Good enough for the fool! He wouldn't even try to save himself." Instead of dying for a Christian ideal or even trying to preserve life in a lost cause, the victim disqualifies himself from our sympathy by dying for a vague aesthetic principle that says: "That which is decorative and of an aesthetic nature must never be used for any other purpose."

As fanatical as it may sound, there are amongst us today those who would disdain to use the performing arts for any other purpose other than the almost purely abstract contemplation of beauty and truth. To these people, drama that is in the least respect practical, moralistic, or didactic can be cast away as utterly unworthy of attention and beneath the dignity of the artist.

Locked in an ideological struggle today, the professedly-Christian world has come face-to-face with the beast that seeks to destroy it. Whether we call this Communism or the all-inclusive secularism, the struggle is clearly a fatal one; yet we disdain to use our drama, our films, and the other narrative arts in a genuine effort to preserve our way of life—our common ideals.

Certainly a great deal of this reticence is occasioned by the ideological tower of Babel, around which we crowd, that makes every man judge subjectively what he should believe and what he should not believe. Our standards and our ideals are not commonly held and a good deal of the public heritage of Christianity left us by our founding fathers has gone down the drain. Secularism is all around us.

There is still a consensus of sorts for which we should be eager to fight—a Christian ideal, a democratic dream—and surely the communicative nature of the theatre should encourage us to use it in the fight. To put the creative talents of our performing artists to work in selling those of our Christian ideals still untarnished—our sense of justice and our ideals of individual freedom—is something worthy and necessary. If we do this with adequate talent and genuine artfulness, it need not demean our art but glorify it.

The other camp is active. Many superbly gifted Marxists, materialists, and nihilists have taken the field against us. We've discussed a half dozen of them in the preceding pages. Other prophets with other messages have been given attention, such as Jean Anouilh, for example, who has peddled, quite repectably, his own cynical brand of world-weariness. Again we've had Beckett, Genet, Albee and the others who have made quite socially acceptable, if not quite comfortable, their nihilistic gabblings about truth and untruth which they seem already to have resigned themselves to find undistinguishable.

We "Christian humanists" seldom speak. We have our poetic religious dramatists and our coterie experimenters. Theirs has been, for the most part, a drama of tea-party cuteness and has made no real attempt to give Christianity the hard-sell treatment Brecht has given some points of Communist doctrine. One need only to read some of Brecht's "lesson plays" to see that even didactic drama—drama that almost literally clubs you over the head with an idea or an outlook—can be written well and effectively if one is talented and not half-hearted about making the effort.

There is undoubtedly a certain primacy for the highest form of art which seeks to recreate—to fill the mind and the heart with sublime thought and feeling. There is, however, a great potential in the film and on the stage for the more practical use of art. The stage can at times be used for a *sort* of teaching and preaching and convincing with clever, well-conceived and dramatically arresting arguments. Shaw demonstrates this as does Brecht and most recently Chayefsky and Bolt. The need for this is an immediate one, for by turning our backs in artistic disdain while the Marthas of the world use the great machine of the stage as a sounding board for their ideas, we serve no one.

Christianity is tremendously more revolutionary and exciting than Marxism. The revolution of love that Christ brought to the world makes Marx's hopelessly optimistic, material promises look like so much corn-meal mush. And yet we steer away from hard Christian drama that demonstrates the dynamism of truth. We restrict that which we apologetically call Catholic or Christian or patriotic drama to pageants of great sweetness and delicate beauty which are far removed from the problem of living as a Christian in a materialistic world. Our attempts at religious drama or patriotic drama retreat into the beautiful groves of poetic abstraction and do not venture forth into the give-and-take arena of the world.

As the times have clearly told us, there are great works to be done in this century. The theatre can provide a magnificent means for spreading the good news of Christianity—of human rights—of justice—of peace—if only we would step down from the pretty marble pedestal of pure, unadulterated art, roll up our sleeves and try.

Finally, it seems to me that there's too much "knocking" and alarm bell ringing going on lately about the American professional theatre. It is fun to jump on the bandwagon and slash away at everything in sight. It seems something rather like a wild revolutionary frenzy, with everyone dashing down to the village square with a candidate for decapitation. "The theatre's no good! The stage is rotten! Theatrical producers are all swindlers, cheats, and perverters of youth! Broadway is on the ropes! It's dead!" Whoa! Wait just a minute!

First of all it's certainly true that America and her theatre have not yet been distinguished by the kiss of real theatrical greatness. Our professional theatre is good—we're notably competent—and now and then we break through into the bright light of really first-rate theatre, but as for great play-wrights, we have had none. Furthermore, there has been a re-trenchment in our theatre since the days when a host of play-houses were operating along the "Great White Way," and in many a choice location in New York a parking lot now gapes where once a theatre stood. Similarly, it's true that genuine act-ing excellence has been all but driven from the stage by the inner-directed incommunicability of the so-called "Method" of the Actor's Studio.

Despite all this, let's turn away from the gloomy side and see what appears on the other side of the ledger. There's no doubt that we have fewer shows inhabiting our theatres than in years past, but what of their quality? Despite the penchant for invective of certain of us facetious reviewers, we have seen some magnificent offerings in the theatre these last few seasons and a fair number of good workman-like pieces of en-tertainment to round things out. Greatness has never grown on trees, and when we look back at the years past, when half a hundred or more shows at a time played Broadway, just how great were they? How many of them could maintain the pace of *A Man For All Seasons, Gideon, The Miracle Worker, My Fair Lady, Fiorello, The Tenth Man, Carnival,* and *Becket?* Surely some of them could, but—lest we forget—a great many of them were inconsequential nothings played with slipshod ineptitude to the same gawking patrons who lose themselves inhumanly in the situation comedies and soap operas of TV. Is this a defeat for the theatre or a retrenchment?

And what of the playwrights? Because O'Neill and Odets and Anderson and Miller and Williams only got part way up the mountain and have stopped short on the near side of great-ness, does this mean that Chayefsky, Mosel, Gibson, and all the other young comers can't make it? A few more years may tell. And does our present paucity of playwrights mean that we will get nothing more from Europe on the order of Bolt and Duerenmatt?

And the "Method"—that wildly optimistic piece of non-sense that suggests that with a smattering of psychology, "in-ner sincerity," and stage movement like that of a herniated baboon, one can plumb the depths of a character's soul—has

been forced to compare its wares with the superb English actors who have of late dominated the American stage with their
skilled technique. This is all to the good. Olivier, Donald
Pleasance, Paul Scofield, Douglas Campbell and others give
our boys and girls a first class example of what a perfect joy
skilled acting can be.

Broadway—the American professional theatre wherever it
may be found—will not, I maintain, go down the drain; and the
main course of our theatre is still pretty much the taste of those
who support the theatre.

And so it goes. Our theatre is just theatre. Those who would
make it over into some sort of cult—looking for sublime religious experience in the playhouse—will be far better off in
"the church of their choice"; those who demand that it be
deathlessly significant *all* the time might do better getting
into politics; those who seek "something for the children" will
do better at the zoo. Our theatre continues to waddle along,
sometimes healthy, sometimes sick and sad, but always hinting
at the brilliance it every once in a while reflects as the world
occasionally shows signs of becoming a better place.

Index

INDEX

Nihil obstat: Edward A. Cerny, S.S.
  Censor Librorum

Imprimatur: Lawrence J. Shehan, D.D.
  Archbishop of Baltimore
March 25, 1962

The *nihil obstat* and *imprimatur* are official declarations that a book or pamphlet is free of doctrinal and moral error. No implication is contained therein that those who have granted the *nihil obstat* and *imprimatur* agree with the opinions expressed.